A Fitter's Life

JOHN EVARDSON

(1921 – 1993)

The Life & Times Of

A Grimsby Marine Engine Fitter

Compiled & Edited by David Evardson

With Song Lyrics and Music Including Contributions
from Bob Pearson & Liam Duffy

1st Edition 1985 (Reprints 1986 & 1987)

Large Print Version 1988

This Edition Copyright © 2015 David Evardson

ISBN: 151738463X
ISBN-13: 978-1517384630

BOOKS BY DAVID EVARDSON

As Dave Evardson:
The Fenwold Riddle
The Fenwold Inheritance

As David Evardson:
Gelding For Beginners

www.DaveEvardson.com

CONTENTS - STORY

CONTENTS - SONGS

EDITOR'S NOTE

The original 1985 edition of 'A Fitter's Life' was the result of many happy hours – over several pints, I may add – of interviewing and recording my Dad's childhood and working life recollections. I know that Dad enjoyed the experience, especially when the local Live Theatre Group skilfully transformed his reminiscences into a musical play entitled 'West Marsh Story'. With songs and music performed by The Little Band (my wife Julie, Max Bradley, Brian Massen and me – aided by Dick Appleton and Bob Pearson) the play enjoyed a couple of short but well received runs taking in several venues in and around Grimsby. Thanks to Sylvia Moss, John Mooney, Mike Payne (R.I.P.) and crew – and especially our friend Martin Campbell for putting us in touch with the company.

Thirty years on, it's time to enhance the original book with more of Dad's jottings, along with all of the songs used in 'West Marsh Story', plus a few others inspired by him.

I would like to dedicate this book to fond memories of Mam and Dad, my sister Sheila and brothers Tom, Chris and John.

The various cartoons were drawn by Dad, except for those on pages 63, 87 and 110 (me) and on page 37 (my brother John).

David Evardson

CHAPTER ONE

OVER THE MARSH

Thursday, 24th March 1921.

"There you are lass," the old midwife said. "A little lad," and she placed the baby into its mother's arms. "Come and have a look at your son then mister. Mind you he's not much to look at."

The child was a tiny thing, about five pounds and like a puny pink monkey. "He'll be lucky if he makes old bones," she sighed, "for he's come into the world with bronchitis."

The infant was gasping for breath in the arms of its anxious mother, but its father looked at his wife with pride. "We have a son at last lass. Aren't we lucky?"

They already had two daughters, Olga and Dorothy, the latter only a year old and Olga just three.

"Wait while the lasses see him. He'll be all right me duck."

I was to get to know that old midwife real well over the next few years, as Mother had babies at regular intervals – nearly enough for a football team!

I can just remember the old house we lived in then, or at least the two rooms we occupied, the dwelling being shared with another family. It was in Hilda Street, off Cleethorpe Road.

Dad was a taxi driver at that time with a firm called Watson's (they were also funeral directors) who had offices near the Dock Crossings. He was very proud of his cab, and used to do all his own running repairs. It was a Daimler, with solid tyres – the first one in the area.

The taxi business then was very profitable, relying as it did on the bumper fishing trips that were the general rule. Most of Dad's customers were fishermen, chiefly skippers and mates, but there'd be deckies as well if landings were especially good.

After being at sea for five or six weeks, risking their lives and working endless hours, their precious shore time would often be taken up with a chartered car and driver, cruising around the town's many pubs and clubs for a well-deserved spree, including a little bit on the side should the chance arise (as it often did).

And then it was back to sea, broke. Or, as the engineer would have it, 'piston broke'.

When I was about four we were allotted a council house – Number Seven, Armstrong Place. It had three bedrooms, a living room downstairs, an outside closet and a coalhouse, plus a scullery with a coal-fired copper that heated water for the bath in the little bathroom in the corner.

The house was situated over the far west side of Grimsby in the neighbourhood known as the West Marsh, so called because it was built over the Humber marshes. It wasn't posh, but the family never minded living 'over the marsh' – we all thought we'd moved into Buckingham Palace!

My sisters and I started our educations at Saint Paul's Church School in Chapman Street, just off Armstrong Street, and we got on very well there.

It would be about December 1927 when Dad lost his job. There were thousands without work, and no hope of getting any. I can well recall the man in the bowler hat, ticking off the prices of our bits of furniture to be sold before we could qualify for relief under the means test. We were left with four chairs and a table. Even our wireless set went, but they didn't attempt to remove the fifty-foot aerial pole that stayed in the back garden as a silent memorial.

But though we didn't have much, we were still able to entertain ourselves. For somehow we managed to hang on to our gramophone – a little brown wind-up box with a big green horn speaker. It used to be the focus of our Sunday nights. One week, my uncle and his family would come to us, and the next week we used to go to their house. Together we would listen to records of Florrie Ford, Harry Tate and all the old timers.

The youngsters in the family would have to give a turn themselves – you know, singing or reciting poetry that you'd learned at school. I used to take off Bing Crosby – I had a good voice then. Then there was Nelson Eddy and Jeanette MacDonald – we used to sing all their songs, from The Chocolate Soldier and other musicals.

We spent many happy hours listening to our old favourites, despite the general gloom that hangs over any house whose breadwinner has no job. And for Christmas dinner that year we had baked cod, done in the oven in the range alongside the fire, with roast potatoes in their jackets, Mother and Father leading us in carols to the old gramophone records. You see, we had our own version of karaoke even then!

From about the age of five I was entrusted to look after my younger brother and two little sisters. Children could run about quite safely then without any fear of being accosted by anyone. And, especially when my Dad was out of work, teatimes would find us among a little crowd of ragamuffins, waiting for the arrival of the workmen's tram from Immingham.

From Immingham Dock there was a tramway through to Immingham Halt – that was on the top of the hill just where the Immingham road ran onto the dock area. It joined the railway line there, then ran under the railway bridge at Pyewipe, and on into Gilbey Road. Here the line branched – one line running over the top and one underneath. That's where most of the dock workers who lived thereabouts used to get off the tram.

And it was here that we nippers would gather at teatimes, waiting to ask the homecoming dockers if they had any bread left from the packing-up their wives had given them for their lunches. Eventually our performance became so regular that they would ask their wives to pack them some extra morsels of bread, sandwiches and what have you. It used to help our families, you see.

At home there was usually not much on the table, and these gifts used to make a meal for four or five of us – they would give us that much bread. You couldn't be too proud to accept such kindness. Nearly everybody was out of work after the First World War. You had to swallow your pride, because many were near to starving.

The official so-called benefits were pitiful really. Families would have to go on the parish. Even then the maximum benefit could only cater for a family of four. But Mother wouldn't see us go hungry if she could help it.

A certain amount of help came from relatives who were in work. My Uncle Bill was working, and so was my Uncle Harry. But Mother used to make it a rule that we bring home any bread we were given. Usually we would have it toasted.

Dad used to keep rabbits in the back garden. He'd knock off one or two of them when it was somebody's birthday or at Christmas time, and he used to skin them straight away in the yard.

You weren't allowed to keep chickens in council houses – you could keep rabbits, but not chickens. You'd try and grow what you could, but the soil around there was worn out. There was no goodness in it. You could dig two feet into the ground, put in your spade and lift it out again, but all you got was powder. I don't know what they gave us gardens for, because even weeds wouldn't grow in ours!

As kids we used to go to old Father Fagan's tin hut in Littlecoates – he ran the Methodist mission there. A good old chap he was, and he formed a children's brass band.

We used to go to St Paul's Church school then, in Chapman Street – St Paul's church was on Corporation Road – and the headmaster was Mr Barraclough. We use to take pennies to school towards the books. We sat on forms, about forty of us, the schoolteacher in the front with a wooden chair.

After the first year they provided us with desks. Not the kind with a lid, just a surface to write on. The first year we had a slate and a slate pencil. For counting we had a bead frame, called an abacus. We also had our own little knick-knacks there, to show us how to lace our boots, made of two bits of card with lace-holes in them.

Once in the art class, we had to take any part of our clothing, put it on our desk, and draw it. I took one of my boots off – there was hardly any sole on it – and I drew it. The teacher was Miss Navenby, an old lady. (She'd be about a hundred and thirty now.) Well, she was quite taken with the picture I drew of my old boot. She had it pinned up on the wall for weeks and weeks. She thought it was marvellous.

For the next week's art class, she brought a fish from the docks, and she told us all to draw it. And the one who drew the best picture could take the fish home for their tea. It was a big fresh cod. Well, I won the fish and took it home, and it made a meal for the whole family.

For a while there was a greyhound track on the site of the tip at Littlecoates, at the end of Elsenham Road. There had been a cow field there, but it was all boggy, so they drained it and put this greyhound track there. Well, I don't know whether much thought had gone into the siting of it, because hardly anyone paid to go in. You only had to walk to the top of the tip, and you'd have a better view of the racing from up there than by paying for admission to the track below. Even the bookies took up positions on top of the tip – there were so many people up there. The track didn't survive very long.

As for politics, the whole area was staunch Labour. At voting time, the kids would parade with placards bearing pictures of the Labour candidate, singing, "Vote, vote, vote for Mr So-and-so." The Conservative canvassers took their lives in their hands if they came knocking on doors over in Little Russia, as the area was sometimes referred to. I remember them coming round one time, the Tory candidate and all his henchmen in a big car with a megaphone, and all the kids surrounded his car and rocked it until it tipped over! They daren't show their faces any more after that.

Remember, this was a council area, where the people had lived most of their working lives, and so naturally they were all Labour voters.

The biggest part of them had fought in the First World War, among the blood and guts and all the rest of it. And coming out of the services after the war, there were no jobs for them. Once the munitions factories had closed down, that was it – unless you went to sea.

The dockers at Immingham were a regular crowd. Oh, you could go to Immingham and stand in the queue if you liked, on the chance of being picked out. But then you couldn't go down to the labour exchange if you stood in the queue. So you had to take potluck. And it was a long walk to Immingham. For if you hadn't a job you certainly had no money for the tram. It would be a walk of several miles along the bank.

I mentioned the usual fare for Christmas dinner was baked cod. I remember having chicken once, and thinking how marvellous it was. That was the first time we'd ever tasted chicken. My mother used to go on the market about ten or eleven o'clock at night just before Christmas. This was when the traders had finished selling, and whatever they had left over they'd be letting go cheap. But eventually everybody twigged on, and she was lucky to come away with anything worthwhile.

She managed to get a duck one year, and a piece of pork, and we thought we'd done very well. She also got some tainted fruit.

The following January, Dad was lucky enough to get a job at Consolidated Fisheries as a lorry driver in their Engineer's Department.

Meanwhile at the bottom of our street the builders had started work on a new school. The local paper reported that the Prince of Wales was visiting the town on a double event – to open the new cantilever-operated Corporation Bridge, and to lay the foundation stone for Armstrong Street School. He would also visit the large Dixon's Paper Mills that day, 19th July 1928. Huge pulp blocks were piled up to make a big stage and seating to see the Prince's retinue come by. He eventually became Edward the Eighth and then (after his abdication) the Duke of Windsor.

I had a very happy childhood as a whole, playing all the normal pranks that lads got up to. I was going fishing one day whilst on school holidays, the venue being the Humber bank over the old tip. I was equipped with a homemade line, fifty foot long with hooks and a heavy lead sinker on the end. My younger brother used to stick to me like a leech, and as usual he trundled along behind me. Walter was his name, but to the family he was Wowwo. (My little sisters – by now I had two more – couldn't get their tongues round 'Walter', so his knickname was used by all and sundry for years.)

Having arrived at the muddy bank with Wowwo behind me, I proceeded to whirl the line and sinker round my head, when suddenly there was a *thump!* and I looked behind me to see my little brother laid unconscious on the shore. A man passing on his bike on the bank bundled him onto his crossbar, and rushed him to the hospital.

No going home for me that day. I daren't, for Wowwo was the apple of Mother's eye, and it would be Dad's belt for me. So I went to my mate Ken Bellamy's house, and slept in their shed that night. I managed to collect enough nerve together to go home the next morning – and what a welcome I got! Mother was tearfully hugging me, and Wowwo was hopping and jumping about with glee, as though nothing had happened to him and I was the injured one. We were pals for life after that, and what a tough nut he turned out to be, as strong as a young ox.

We used to play football and cricket in the street, and often had a twang across the arse from the local bobby, not for playing ball games, but for running across the road without looking. He often joined in for a kick around when there was no traffic. We all feared yet respected the local copper on the beat. He did a lot of excellent social work all off the cuff.

We liked the cold October and November nights for our spirited mischief. Horse and cart was the main means of transport for the local tradesmen, and 'oss-toddin' used to be a profitable job for us lads. We used to earn quite a bit of money collecting this free by-product from the many tradesmen's horses that plied Grimsby's streets at that time. The allotment gardeners in the area gladly paid for this fine fertiliser. We'd keep it in the yard while Saturday, then cart it round in a wheelbarrow. We used to all join in, all the neighbours, and all the kids. Most of the money would go to Mam to put a bit more food on the table, but we youngsters would save the odd coppers to buy fireworks for the Great Night. One or two of these, I've got to admit, were used for tantalising the locals.

There was one man who had a row of full-hearted cabbages in his garden. Some naughty lads inserted a little demon (exploding cracker) in the centre of each plant – and the poor bloke ended up with the finest set of stalks in existence! As for the culprits, well of course they collected the reddest smarting backsides they'd ever had. (I speak from first hand experience!)

What with window tapping, door-knob-tying, etcetera, my mates and I became the scourge of the district.

Another escapade we got up to involved a nice length of coloured ribbon and a lovely big sheet of brown paper. We lay the paper on an opened-up cardboard box to keep it clean, and then one of the lads looked around till he'd found a really big dollop of dog-dirt. He brought it back on a shovel and placed it exactly in the middle of the sheet of paper. Next we folded it into a nice, neat parcel, and tied it up with the beautiful coloured ribbon, and left it just outside someone's front gate.

Eventually a young woman would walk up, see the exquisite looking package, look both ways, then pick it up and slide it craftily into her basket. Although we were all hidden out of sight, we could clearly see the young woman looking round furtively before scurrying into her house. After a few moments the undone stinking parcel came flying out of the door, a shrill voice yelling out, "You dirty young sods! If I find out who did it I'll bloody strangle him!" Wowwo and I were usually the main suspects. I can't think why.

I was pretty bright at school and got on quite well with the teachers. But it seemed funny to me that, every time someone's bike tyres were let down, I was always given the job of pumping them up again. I often wondered who was splitting on me.

I was in Standard 7A, which was top of the school, when I was eleven years old, and had passed my examination for the scholarship, which meant that I could go to the grammar school. It was called Wintringham and was situated in stately buildings on Eleanor Street not far from the town centre, a pay school where the local nobs paid for their sons to go. However my scholarship award entitled me to only part of the money required to secure a place, and Dad said that he couldn't afford the rest of the fee.

So I carried on at Armstrong. I was happy about that, because it was a happy school. Fine teachers – Mr. Potter the headmaster, Mr. Queue his second-in-command taking higher maths and English (also first aid), 'Daddy' Bristow as maths teacher, Mr. Warburton on geography and history, Mr. Aby teaching science and Mr. Potts as sports master (and a very good cricketer). All in all they were a very fine team, so you see, in my opinion I missed out on nothing in my education, especially since I was to begin my instruction again at fourteen in engineering.

Dad took me on one side one night and told me all about the facts of life. I made out I didn't know, but the gooseberry bush myth had been buried a long time before that.

The next day being Monday, I ran out of school at four o'clock, as I knew that Mam had pawned something and would want her shopping doing. She could only spare two bob. The usual ritual was to get the big bass out of the lobby, and go through my normal fashion of asking her what to get.

"We must have some bread," she said, "and cakes and eggs and a bit of bacon, if you can get it. Your Dad will be famished when he comes home. Get what you can."

How could it be done on two bob? Times were very hard and we were nearly always on the brink of poverty, even with Dad working. He was on twenty-six shillings a week, and there was no such thing as family allowance. But Mam knew what she was doing – and so did I. I could put the act on very well, and we always managed to keep ourselves well fed.

First I went to Melia's on Corporation Road.

I was short for my age, so I peered over the counter in all my ragged attire, and with a natural hungry look. "Can I have three pen'orth of bacon bits please mister, as we have nothing in the house to eat?"

I fumbled the heavy coins in my pocket. Mam had given me all the two bob in coppers, so that I never brandished silver into the man's face.

"You look as though you could do with some fattening up lad," he said as he piled the bits up from the side of the slicer. "There's a nice ham bone in there as well. Tell Mam it will make some lovely broth."

I forced tears into my eyes and said with a sob, "Thank you mister. You don't happen to have some cracked eggs or broken biscuits, do you?"

The shopkeeper frowned with pity. "It's about time they got this bloody party out. Ramsay MacDonald and his lot will never do you lot any good. Cuts in wages indeed! And you look as if you could do with a good meal or two. Poor little lad!"

I thought to myself, "I wish he'd bloody hurry up – all these sodding coppers in my pocket weigh a ton!" He took the bass and lovingly piled in a big parcel of bacon, a bag of broken biscuits and about two dozen cracked eggs.

"How much is that mister?"

"Give me a shilling son," he said, "but don't come back again 'cos we can't afford it."

The tradesmen were saints in those days. I counted out twelve hot pennies into his hand and then ambled over to Glenton's for two penny ducks. They call them faggots these days, but they were four times as big, and a lot tastier.

"And can I have some pork crackling please?"

"How many are in your house?" asked the lady behind the counter.

"Eight of us," I said. So she made me up a huge packet for no charge. That was one and two I'd spent, and the bass was half full. Then I carried on to the baker's shop for my stale bread.

"Yes sonny?" the woman said.

"Could you let me have some stale bread and pastries please missus, as we have nothing in the house to eat?" I pleaded pathetically.

"Of course we can my little angel," she replied, and loaded bread and cakes into my bass till it was full. "There, take that home to your Mam. She'll know what to do with it."

That lot cost me three pence, so I had seven pence left over to give to Mam. Off I went home, dragging the laden bass behind me.

Mam took the bread, white and brown, out of the bass and put it into a big bowl, and let the cold water tap run on it till it was all soaked. Then she carefully placed the lot in the oven, and we had what tasted like fresh bread for our tea – you couldn't tell the difference – with bacon and eggs and crackling (which we all loved), and a mug of tea to wash it down with. There was always a tin of condensed milk on the table, which we would spread on our dry bread for afters, and then stagger away from the table like fighting cocks!

Families like ours had to know where to go to find food that was cheap or even free, and of course, Grimsby being in its heyday, fish was usually plentiful, and therefore an important part of our diet.

In the herring season on the Fish Docks, the drifters used to come in and land their catches, about forty or fifty boats at a time. This was in the dock basin. Sometimes the catches were so prolific that you could go down with your bass, and ask a deck-hand to fill it – for nothing, as they would never take money from kids. We would then go into town to sell them for six-a-penny, and made quite a thriving business of it, for a full fish bass could hold about a hundred of the little silver fish. Yet we made sure we'd enough left over for the family's needs.

We also used to go to the River Head, which was the dead-end of the Alexandra Dock, and backed into Victoria Street, near the town centre. The River Freshney also runs into it from the Alexandra Road end. The river was also known as the Haven by the inhabitants of the West Marsh, where it ran past South Parade School and through the Duke of York Gardens, called the Boulevard by the locals, or the Bully by the kids. The little river came into town via the Willows and Littlecoates, rising originally in the Lincolnshire Wolds. There it is fed from natural springs, the main one being at the village of Croxby, close to the well-known beauty spot of Ravendale Valley.

The River Head itself was the centre of much trade, most of which consisted of barge cargoes – grain, fruit, nuts and cattle food, etcetera. We liked it especially when they were unloading tiger nuts, peanuts or locusts, which were a great favourite amongst us young urchins, and I believe their nutritional value was second to none.

We also went scrumping in Tickler's orchards, and swimming bare buff in the Willows, all the tomboy girls joining in with gusto. The time passed away quickly for us, and I am sure that, as full-blooded life-loving kids, we enjoyed every precious minute of our adolescent youth, all the innocent amusement made with our parents and friends, with no mechanical stimulants or substitutes.

I recall one particular instance, when my pal and I were at a loose end one day.

He had a wicked sense of humour. He says to me, "Hey John, I've got a good idea. Come with me, and we'll have a bit of fun. You know that cow field at the end of Macaulay Street? There's some lovely big cow-pats there. Get a shovel and fetch it along."

So we managed to ease a nice big one onto the shovel, and carefully carried it back to our street. He says, "I've got my Dad's old bowler hat here. By, we're gonna have some fun!"

When he explained the plan to me I had to agree it was a stroke of genius. We placed the cow-pat on the pavement while the area was deserted, and covered it with his father's hat. Then we waited while a woman came past, and stopped to ask us, "What are you little devils up to, holding that hat down like that?"

My mate says, "Our canary got out missis, and we've caught it under this hat. We won't half cop it if we don't get it home again." It was a hot day and it was starting to whiff a bit. By this time a little crowd of women had accumulated. (You know how inquisitive they can be – they don't want to be left out of anything.) So when they were all paying attention I explained, "We reckon the best thing to do is for a few of you to crouch down, and when we lift the hat, all concentrate on grabbing the bird."

How the hell they didn't catch the stink, I'll never know. Perhaps because they were so excited. Anyway, up came the hat.

And down went the women.

What a bloody mess! You've never seen owt like it in your life, and we ran like bats out of hell.

That night, when Dad got home, of course I got the belt, but it was well worth the punishment. By this time I was used to it.

That was the worst of our escapades – honestly. Though, of course, we were little angels at home, for most of the time anyway. Usually when we'd been out all day making mischief, arriving home for tea, Mam would be ready with the question, "And where do you think you've been?" To which the stock answer would be, "Only eggin' Mam, back o' Doig's!"

Doig's was a shipbuilding and repair firm on the docks, behind whose premises you could go collecting seagulls' eggs – as well as getting up to other antics. This phrase was always the stock reply over the marsh whenever someone was asked what they'd been up to, and I'm sure "Eggin' back o' Doig's" covered a multitude of sins!

Not quite all of our amusement was purely of our own making though. There was the cinema. They used to make it worth your while to go to the pictures, especially at the Chantry where we used to go. The picture house was on Chantry Lane, and it cost just three ha'pence to get in. The manager was a good bloke, he was. And all of us kids from families that didn't have much (I wouldn't say we were paupers) used to go there for what was known as the tuppenny rush. Though, as I say, it didn't quite cost that much to go in. Yet he always gave us a bag of goodies and an orange to take in, so he can't have been making that much out of us.

We would have two good hours of entertainment, with Our Gang, the Keystone Cops, adventures with heroine Pearl White, or Buster Keaton, Harold Lloyd and Chester Conklin, to just mention a few. Their escapades were great fantasies that for a brief moment lifted us out of our everyday lives. And our parents must have been pleased that we were kept out of mischief for a while.

But the thrills of the picture house were as nothing compared to my first real experience of living away from home. For very soon I was to embark upon a little adventure of my own.

HAVE YOU ANY PACKING-UP LEFT MISTER?

Every evening at the Pyewipe tram stop
On the Immingham to Grimsby line
There's a little band of urchins waiting
For the clatter of the five-o-nine
And the dockers who've been all day working
Have to chuckle as the stop draws near
For their regular reception party
And the chorus that they always hear

Chorus: Have you any packing-up left Mister?
Just a little bit of bread to share
We've got nothing on our table Mister
Have you anything that you can spare?
Have you any packing-up left Mister?
Have a look inside your box and see
Just a crust or a cob till me Dad gets a job
Then you'll never hear no more from me

In the middle of the nineteen-twenties
There was hardly any work around
And the dockers who had jobs were thankful
They'd enough to keep their fam'lies sound
So they'd save a little snap not eaten
For the kiddies in the West Marsh queue
Cos whenever hungry eyes are pleading
What's a tender-hearted man to do?

When she packs him up for work each morning
And before she sends him on his way
Being grateful that her husband's working
And can bring her home some decent pay
For there's many others on the dole queue
Many families are on the skids
So she packs him up some extra slices
For that little band of West Marsh kids

Now we've put a lot of years behind us
And the bad old days should all be gone
But have seventy-odd years of progress
Really brought us any further on?
For there's just as many folk not working
And nobody seems to give a damn
Generosity now comes by giro
And there isn't any Pyewipe tram

HAVE YOU ANY PACKING-UP LEFT MISTER?

A VISIT TO THE PAWNSHOP
(Bob Pearson)

Saturday is wages day, a-shopping we will go
With a visit to the pawnshop to pay off all we owe
He's got his suit and watch back, so tonight we'll have a jar
You'll see us in the Albion a-propping up the bar

Chorus
So it's round and round the carousel and it never seems to end
We've just pulled through another week and we are on the mend
For we've redeemed our treasures and we've evened up the score
But it won't be long before we will be pawning them once more

I love me Sunday dinner, I look forward to me meat
Beef two veg and Yorkshire pud don't half go down a treat
And then I put me feet up and I snooze till quart' to four
Cos tomorrow mornin' half past five it's off to work once more

She's packed him up with all the bits left over from their feast
Shoppin's not much fun now buying things that cost the least
She's goin' to the pawnshop to pawn his suit so dear
If she doesn't pay the rent man they'll be slung out on their ear

I hate to see me watch go, it was all me father had
For workin' on the railway through good times and through bad
I'll send her off to pawn it for we won't get through without
She'll get next to nothin' for it but it's better than a clout

The kids have been out shoppin' and they've got a tale to tell
They've scrounged stale bread and bacon bits and some cracked eggs
    as well
We'll have a feast tonight duck, that'll keep you right till morn
It's a bugger that tomorrow we'll need summat else to pawn

She pawned her wedding band today, the first time in her life
Her finger seems so empty but I know she's still me wife
But thinkin' of tomorrow will ease away the pain
For she'll buy it back at one o'clock for it's wages day again

A VISIT TO THE PAWNSHOP

Verse:
Sat-ur-day is wag-es day, a - shopp-ing we will go. With a vis-it to the
pawn shop, to pay off all we owe. He's got his suit and watch back, so tonight we'll have a jar. You'll see us in the Al-bi-on, a - prop-ping up the bar. And it's

Chorus:
round and round the car-ou-sel, and it nev-er seems to end. We've just pulled through an-
oth-er week and we are on the mend. For we've re-deemed our treas-ures, and we've
ev-ened up the score. But it won't be long be-fore we will be pawn-ing them once
more.

EGGIN' BACK O' DOIG'S

While growin' up in Grimsby we was just like any kids
With hide and seek and knock-door-run and pinchin' dustbin lids
To our mothers we was angels, never naughty girls and boys
When they'd ask what we'd been up to, we'd say:
"Eggin' back o'Doig's"

<u>Refrain</u>
Eggin' back o' Doig's, we're only eggin' back o' Doig's
When they'd ask what we'd been up to, we'd say:
"Eggin' back o'Doig's"

A grumpy gardener down our street had grown some lovely blooms
When Bonfire Night came he ran out to flashes, bangs and booms
Smokin' stalks was all he found left of his pride and joys
But it wasn't 'owt to do wi' me, I was
Eggin' back o' Doig's

Me and me pals was always up to summats for a lark
And once or twice I must admit I overstepped the mark
That's when me Dad would tek his belt out of his corduroys
And I'd receive a pastin' for
Eggin' back o' Doig's

A toffee-nosed young woman found a parcel by her gate
And as she slyly took it in we hid to watch and wait
Then angrily she flung it out – she'd lost her stuck-up poise
'Twas a smelly lump of troddle we'd found
Eggin' back o' Doig's

My elder sister tied the knot when I was still a lad
I hadn't had the birds and bees explained yet by me Dad
When she produced my little nephew I was overjoyed
When I asked her how she got him she said:
"Eggin'back o' Doig's"

Our pleasures all were simple as the years of childhood sped
Swimmin' bare-buff in the Willows, fishin' in the River Head
And though the youngsters of today have many finer toys
They couldn't have more fun than we had
Eggin' back o' Doig's!

EGGIN' BACK O' DOIG'S

Verse:
While grow-in' up in Grims-by, we was just like an-y kids, With hide and seek and knock-door-run and pinch-in' dust-bin lids. To our moth-ers we was an-gels, nev-er naught-y girls and boys; When they'd ask what we'd been up to, we'd say: "Egg-in' back o' Doig's!"

Refrain:
Egg-in' back o' Doig's, we're on-ly egg-in' back o' Doigs; When they'd ask what we'd been up to, we'd say "Egg-in' back o' Doig's!"

CHAPTER TWO

THROUGH THE LOCK GATES

When I was just turned twelve years old, Dad managed to place me on a pleasure trip arranged through his employers, Consolidated Fisheries. I was signed on under insurance articles, and it cost my father half-a-crown.

The ship was the Bellona, a North Sea steam trawler, owned privately by Lady Marsden, the wife of the company's managing director. The vessel was immaculate, with a specially picked crew who had sailed in her for years. She was kept scrubbed down from stem to stern, with polished brass and all the rest and, oh yes, even carpets in the engine room! For if at any time Her Ladyship should want to inspect her ship, it had to be in spick and span order.

The way it was sprung on me was like this. My Dad says to me, "Look lad, all my family's been to sea. We're all a seafaring family. How would you like to go to sea for a holiday?"

It being the school summer holidays. Well, I was a weedy little fellow. There was nothing on me, and I was always ailing (remember, I was born with bronchitis). So, Dad thought it might do me good. That was the way he put it to me.

It was August, and the weather was grand. In those times it seemed you could always rely on August being hot, with the tar bubbling on the roads and the water carts having to come and cool them down, all the kids running alongside barefoot and shirtless and brown as berries, keeping pace all the way and having a great time. But I was more than willing to forego these pleasures for a few weeks, eager to savour this new experience.

Of course the days crawled by then, until at last it was time to leave. Approaching the ship I must have looked a comical sight. I had a standard kit bag of course, and it was actually bigger than me. I had to drag it, for there was no chance of lifting it. Somehow I managed to get the bag and myself on board, and looked around for the skipper.

His name was Esra Allen, a Cleethorpes man and, I believe, a staunch Methodist. He was an upstanding citizen and very well respected. When I found him and introduced myself, he said that I would be sleeping in his berth. The sleeping arrangement was simple. He slept in his bunk, and I slept on the floor. This seemed fine except (as I was to discover later) every time the ship rolled, I would roll with it right under his bunk, then on the return of the roll I would end up on the opposite side of the berth.

When we'd been sailing for only a few hours, Esra comes up to me and asks, "How are you doing then sonny?"

"I feel all right," I replied.

"Well, you should be. We're only in the river."

Then, as we got out of the Humber, and just turning the corner, I started being seasick. I felt as if I wanted to be dead, and was convinced that my end had come. I was laid on the casing next to the funnel, the warmest place to be, and it seemed to be raining cats and dogs. In fact, it was only the wash from the waves, blowing onto the casing top.

Esra comes up to me again. "You look green lad. What's up with you?"

I groaned, "I don't know. I feel poorly."

"Well," he suggested, "go and see the cook and ask him if he's got owt that'll cure you."

"I daren't climb down from here," I protested. "I might go over the side."

So he called to the mate, "Take him along to the steward and see what he's got."

The cook was from Jamaica, and the mate presented me to him. "Will you look after this lad Cookie? He's not feeling too well," and winked at him.

"Alright boss," he says, "I'll get some of this old streaky bacon out."

With that I started being ill straight away. As I lay there in the galley companionway, I said nothing, but thought, "He's done me a lot of bloody good, he has!"

Next he said, "Come with me."

He took me back to the casing top, above the galley where there was a wooden drum where he pickled beef with saltpetre. He hauled a lump of beef out, and it looked a lovely shade of green. My own colour must have been trying hard to match it, and immediately I started again. The broad white flash of his grin told me he was having fun at my expense. But then, thinking back to pranks I'd played on others, I couldn't very well blame him, could I?

At last he took pity on me, and led me back to the galley where he gave me a mug of broth.

"Get that down you," he said.

I did, and surprisingly I kept it down. With it he gave me some hard cabin biscuits. These were about a quarter of an inch thick, and I'm not kidding you, you could have nailed them to the wall and used them as plaques if they were painted up. They were that hard.

"Now soak them in the broth," he said.

Well, I never did get them properly soaked; the broth never got through them. They were made by Watmough's, and later on, during the war, we called them dog biscuits - there's only a dog could bite through them!

He was quite a character, that old cook, and he was a good cook too. One morning early, one of the deckhands, creeping up to the galley, woke the Jamaican, whose hearing must have been very good.

He yelled out, "Who am dat up dere wid de bare feet on?"

Down came the reply. "Only me Sambo, mekkin' some toast."

"Who am me?"

"I'm one of the deckies."

"Well, get out of my bloody galley, else I'll cuff your earholes!"

We soon got amongst the fish on the Dogger Bank, so the skipper said to the cook, "Will you come and give us a hand in the pound to gut some fish?"

The deck was laden. The skipper was afraid they wouldn't get rid of them down the hold in time for the next haul. This was when the Dogger Bank was flourishing with haddock and cod. So the cook started gutting along with the deckies.

One of the deckies was on the bridge, giving a hand with the steering. He caught sight of old Sam gutting there, the big, brawny black man that he was, hard as nails and strong as any two men on board. Gutting was going on at a tremendous rate, hearts, guts and livers flying across the deck. The deckie picked up a heavy iron shackle and hurled it directly at Sam, shouting, "Come on Sam, you're slowing down!"

Well, the shackle hit old Sam right at the back of the ear, landing with some force. The tough West Indian just straightened up for a moment, shook his head and, flashing the whites of his eyes accusingly, yelled out, "Who frew dat libber?" And then carried on gutting.

I'll not forget old Sam. He'd soon got me onto proper food, having cured me of my seasickness. And, though the weather was stormy as soon as we'd left the Humber, I enjoyed the trip immensely. The weather stayed bad right until we landed, funnily enough.

When we did land, it turned out to be a bumper trip. The catch fetched eight hundred pounds, and that was a lot of cash. The crew had treated me as their mascot, and they all clubbed together and gave me a pile of coins to put in my pocket, about three pounds. Feeling rich and happy, with my kit bag perched on my back, I stepped confidently ashore.

The ground came up to meet me. I'd still got my sea legs, you see, and now that I was back on land, I didn't seem to know what to do with them. By heck, it's a queer sensation till you get used to it.

I managed to get my bag to Riby Square to catch a tram home. When one came, being the little nipper that I was, I had a job lifting my kit bag onto the platform, so the conductor gave me a helping hand with my load.

"How the hell are you going to get this home sonny? Where you bin, Newfoundland?"

"No," I replied. "Only to the Dogger Bank."

"Did you get there on your own?" he cracked. Then I knew he was pulling my leg. "Did you bring me a bit of fish?"

"No, I didn't," I shrugged.

"Never mind," he said kindly. "I'll see you off all right."

So he put me off at the Palace Theatre corner, near Corporation Road, and I walked over the bridge, dragging my bag behind me, and somehow succeeded in getting it home to our house in Armstrong Place. Of course the three pounds went straight into the household kitty, but I didn't mind. I'd just had an amazing holiday that I'd never forget.

I must have acquired some sort of taste on my North Sea voyage for ships and the sea, for the following year saw me on another pleasure trip, but this time all the way to the Icelandic fishing grounds. I was to be in the care of my Uncle Alf, who was second engineer on a trawler called the Florio. She was a bigger vessel than the Bellona, with a whaleback, in contrast with the hurricaned deck of my previous ship.

Uncle Alf had his chief engineer's certificate, and accepted the berth as second when there was no chief's position vacant. He'd taken a liking to the trawler and crew and, despite being offered the position of chief on other ships since joining it, he preferred to remain as second with the ship he liked. So he'd been with the Florio for a few years.

My accommodation this time was in the cabin aft, which had three berths, for the mate, chief and second engineers. In the middle, above the provision lockers, was a big cabin table. This was fitted with racking laths, to stop dinner plates and drinking mugs from sliding all over the place when the ship was pitching and rolling in the heavy seas. The tops of the lockers around the table were covered with padded cushions, and served as seats. Above these were the bunks, with sliding curtains and panel doors, and it was one of these bunks that I was to make my own for the trip, and very comfortable it was too.

We left the North Wall at Grimsby at three in the morning, and so began my first long voyage. There were quite a few ships leaving at the same time, and off we set through the lock gates and into the river, then out into the North Sea.

My Uncle Alf having first watch, I was down the engine room with him. The telegraph was ringing and registering full speed ahead.

No sign of any seasickness for me this time, as I'd already got my sea legs from my previous trip. In any case I was far too fascinated to think about being ill. What a joy it was to see those big engines swishing round, the great piston rods and connecting rods striding round like three great shire horses. I think that experience gave me my everlasting love for steam engines.

I helped down the engine room for two or three days, oiling round and polishing brass work and generally making myself useful. The days seemed to run into one another, so I don't remember just how long into the voyage we were, when the skipper blew down the engine room voice pipe, asking the engineer to turn on the winch steam on the boiler top. We were then off the coast of Iceland, and about to shoot the trawl.

That meant that all the deckhands had to manhandle the nets over the side, and attach the big warp wires to the trawl, paying it out with the winch so that it was trailing a few fathoms from the bottom, and a few hundred yards behind the ship.

After the trawl was shot the crew had a few hours to wait for a good tow. One of the deck hands got out a squeeze box, and we had a fine sing-song on the foredeck, while a few of them were taking the battens and tarpaulins off the fish room hatches.

I had returned below and was occupied pumping out the bilges with one of the steam pumps known as 'donkeys', aptly named for their obstinacy in picking water up straight away, when the skipper blew down again. This time it was to ask me if I'd like to see the trawl and cod end being hauled. Perhaps I could even give a hand with the gutting and stowing.

I finished what I was doing first. When I eventually appeared on deck they had already got the wings of the net on board, and were just swinging the cod end inboard. The third hand stood under the cod end with his thigh-boots, oil frock and sou'-wester on, about to untie the knot. It was a sight that left me goggle-eyed, for the man seemed so small, standing straddle-legged under that massive bag.

Then at an instant it seemed that hundreds of big fish spewed out all over that one part of the deck, where the fish pounds were quartered off with deck boards anchored into stanchions. He never missed one of the fish, and I thought they would beat his body to pulp. However he was a strong man, and backed away with a smile as he yelled out, "A double bag lads! Let's get them sorted out and gutted!"

They sorted them out and started gutting. Cod, halibut, plaice, skate, oh and it seemed to me, every kind of fish in the sea – it was thrilling!

"Come on lad. Grab a knife and get hold of that cod!"

But that was my undoing. The fish was about three feet long. I got hold of its tail and it gave such an almighty twist that I was flung right across the deck. I picked myself up, and did the only thing I could to retain my dignity. I got stuck in again with the rest of the men. With the deckhands' laughter still ringing in my ears, and every bone in my body aching, I started on some smaller ones.

When nearly all the fish had been gutted, the mate patted me on the head and said, "You're a good lad. Before we shoot the trawl again, I'll show you something you'll remember all your life."

He took one of the remaining cod and with his gutting knife removed the heart and liver. Then he laid the heart on the battened-down hatch and said, "Can you see it beating? That will carry on beating till sunset. That's a mystery no-one has ever fathomed out." What he said was right. I'd learned a fisherman's secret.

I helped down the engine room all the rest of the trip, apart from the few times, during fine weather, when the skipper let me take the wheel for a spell. We were full up with fish and expected to make a good trip.

When we got into the river, just in time for the lock gates to open, the section tug came alongside and gave us our number to go in. We were number two. We sailed through the lock pits to our berth on the Pontoon, called 'Pneumonia' by the workers, as it was always bitterly cold.

Ironically, after all the hard work and making a very good catch, we docked to find that there was a glut on the market. Consequently prices were rock bottom and the ship only just managed to clear its expenses, and the unsold fish had to go at giveaway prices to the fishmeal factory for fertiliser. The trawler owners didn't lose out entirely, since of course they had a vested interest in the fishmeal trade.

It was commonly known on the docks that there were about forty trawler owners who, let's give credit where it's due, made the Grimsby trawling fleet the biggest in the world. Great Grimsby was renowned universally as the world's foremost fishing port, and the 'Great' was truly deserved. That these same trawler owners were known throughout the industry as the 'Forty Thieves' was due to the apparently heartless attitude they had towards their workforce.

The poor bloody fishermen were working at times twenty-four hours a day, for as little as three-ha'pence an hour or even less. And it seems an amazing fact now and hard to believe, but as soon as a man was lost overboard or injured, his name was at that instant struck off the payroll, and his family put in jeopardy. It was then up to the Seamen's Missions and similar associations to help them.

Trawler owners would have nothing to do with unions for trawlermen in those times. The work of the town centred almost wholly on fishing. The only other industries to speak of were Hewitt's Brewery, Tickler's Jam Factory and Watmough's Biscuit Factory, and then all the ancillary trades connected with fishing. With such a limited choice of occupations it was a brave or reckless man who tried to fight the system. Though it meant facing terrible dangers, and receiving a pittance in return for their hard work and skill, most fishermen had to be content to stay at sea all their lives, and thought themselves fortunate.

Others weren't so lucky. Later on, when war broke out, my Uncle Alf was to join a boom defence ship, patrolling the Humber estuary and making periodic checks on the boom defence nets, which were positioned to prevent 'U' boats from entering the Humber shipping roads. The ship was an ordinary North Sea trawler, with a twelve-pounder gun mounted on the casing top between the galley and the funnel, the mounting staging straddling the engine room skylights. As you can imagine, there wasn't much horizontal angle that could be used, although it was on a revolving platform - unless you shot your own funnel or wheelhouse down! But they were an effective enough defensive weapon at the time.

Investigating on the North Sea side of the boom one night in the summer of 1941, the ship was sunk with the loss of all hands, and none of the crew, nor any wreckage, was ever found.

Uncle Alf had introduced me to engineering, and that trip with him on the Florio had sparked off a lifelong interest in mechanical things. It had also instilled in me a great respect for the hardworking fishermen I'd sailed with.

You hear a lot about miners and their hardships, and believe me I don't want to underrate in any way the rigours of their trade. But there have been miners that have come to Grimsby and tried trawling, and packed it in after their first trip, being unable to adapt to the different types of austerities. Trawlermen are a breed on their own, tough industrious men, completely dedicated to their arduous life.

Yet despite all the dangers and privations, you seldom heard a fisherman complain about his work. If his wife nagged at him to get a shore job, even if he thought there was any chance of finding one, his reply would usually be something like, "All right duck, but I'll just do one more trip first."

They seem to have been drawn to the sea in a strange way, and the comradeship aboard a trawler when you knew the efforts of every last man and boy were vital for the survival of the ship and crew. It was a life that soon turned lads into men, and hard men too.

I've seen men with calluses on their hands, so hard that they could hammer six-inch nails into the deck with their palms. I'm not joking - ice, ropes, nets and salt water to garnish the blisters made them develop skin on their hands like a rhino's hide.

Talking about ice, I've seen ships come in from sea with their rigging, stays and ratlines about a foot thick with the stuff. The crew had been working all the time chopping ice away throughout the return journey from Iceland. The temperature was so low that the seas froze as they hit the decks. Hands would freeze to ropes and rails, tearing the skin as they were painfully prised away. The cook, taking a mug of steaming hot tea to the bridge, was lucky if there wasn't a film of ice on it by the time it was delivered, and many were heard to say, "The skipper's thanks fell frozen at his feet."

All the trawler's crew would be armed with special hardened-bladed axes, which under bad conditions they had to use if they wanted to see Grimsby again. They were designed for chopping the ice away and for cutting the steel wire warps if the trawl gear became fast on the bottom. For apart from ice there was the other hazard of wreckage unmarked on the charts. The seabed would of course already be charted, but the fishing grounds were like a tremendous scrap yard over the full area of the Arctic Circle. Just imagine fish rooms full of fish and ice, a dead weight, then all the water coming aboard, thirty foot waves from the deck to mast head, freezing solid like an iceberg. So it was a case of communal survival twenty-four hours of every day. Otherwise the ship could so easily run under, or turn turtle with the weight of the ice built up on her superstructure.

I've seen crews coming into port absolutely dead on their feet – they hadn't even had time to wash or shave since leaving the fishing grounds. And then, to cap it all, the markets being over-supplied with fish, they had to settle in debt. After all that soul-destroying work only to come into dock owing the owners money. It was pitiful.

And even landing with a bumper catch, the ordinary trawlerman couldn't be certain of his fair reward. After the ship's expenses were covered, each crew member was entitled to a share in the landing's profit, though for a simple deckhand this was a very meagre percentage.

The profit would depend not only, as I said earlier, on a good market, or on the quantity caught, but also on the quality of fish landed. In a good market the prime fish – the last trawl, so the freshest – could fetch very good prices indeed, and a deckie would rightly look forward to his small share in return for risking his life.

But I used to hear stories of ships coming in to a good market, loaded with fish, only to be greeted by fleets of owners' lorries to take off the prime fish before the catch could be officially landed and tallied. Destined for a private market, this fish would be left out of the reckoning when the crew's share was worked out. And if the cheated fishermen protested, they'd find themselves blacklisted. Better to stay silent, and be grateful for the pittance that the 'Forty Thieves' granted them – at least they had jobs and the means to support their loved ones.

They went in for large families in those days. Wives worked very hard bringing them up (and they didn't make a bad job of it). No vacuum cleaners, dishwashers or washing machines then – just dolly tubs, dolly pegs, big iron wooden-rollered wringers and a lot of sheer backbreaking work. Then there was all the ironing, with the old cast flat-iron that was generally heated on the old Yorkshire range hob.

When men went to sea they were away for four or five weeks at a time, for the trawlers were not so powerful as they later became. The wives drew a small wage every week from the owner, which was deducted from the final settlement at the end of the trip. The schools in Grimsby and Cleethorpes used to close at half-past-one on Fridays – this was so that the youngsters could go 'down dock' to collect their fathers' wages. Each week there was a great competition to get to the different trawler owners' offices first, as the queues would be gigantic. And so this weekly ritual became known as the 'Fish Dock Races'.

As I said, if the trawler settled in debt by making a loss on the trip, money was owed to the owners, so as soon as Dad went back to sea his best suit and shoes went straight into pawn. There were as many pawnshops in Grimsby and Cleethorpes as there were pubs. They were a big help to families who were on the brink of poverty. Not many kids ever had proper shoes or boots on their feet or new clothes. Mostly they would have to make do with their mother's old lace-up boots, and Dad's old trousers with the legs cut down.

Times were bad not just for fishermen's families. Most of the work in the two towns was strongly linked with fishing, so everyone's livelihood depended either directly or indirectly on the success of the main industry.

As hard as they were, the years of the 1920's and 30's saw the continuing build-up of the different fleets. To match this expansion there was a need for highly skilled shore maintenance workers. These craftsmen were nearly as badly paid as the fishermen.

It wasn't easy for the humble deckhand to improve his position. By hard graft and gaining experience he might eventually earn promotion to third hand, especially if he stayed with the same ship and waited for the job to fall vacant. Then if he wanted to progress further, he would have to take trips off without pay and study at Nautical School for his mate's certificate or 'ticket'. More studying was needed for a skipper's ticket. But the most important qualification was years of experience. Without that ingredient no trawlerman could hope to become the master of a ship.

A good skipper aided his career by keeping a diary of every sounding taken with the date, time and position. In a few years he had compiled a book that was worth a fortune. If he had turned in decent trips the information he had gathered would be in great demand when he retired. Usually the diaries were handed down from father to son.

If a trawlerman was mechanically minded, he might set his sights on a career in the engine room. Below decks, he would start as a lowly trimmer, who kept the huge stocks of coal and ice 'trimmed' to maintain the vessel's stability. A trimmer could progress to fireman looking after the boilers. Then it was a question of studying if he wanted to gain his second engineer's and chief's tickets. But again, many years of experience were required to make a chief engineer.

The engine room was the ship's powerhouse and must be maintained in first-class working order. It provided power not only to drive the ship's engines and winches. The old trawlers were illuminated by gas inside and on deck. The gas was generated down the engine room by a gasometer fed by calcium carbide and water, which with the correct burners and lamps gave off a good white light all over the ship.

If a trawler happened to break down then the engineer would have to make quick repairs or, if heavy seas were running, make for the nearest lea and trust to luck. If extensive repairs were necessary, or spares weren't available on board, the ship would have to limp back to port. Then it would be the fitter's job to put things right.

After my trip on the Florio, I started to show a leaning towards mechanical things, and I suppose it was inevitable from that point in time that a fitter's life was to be my calling.

I'd always wanted a bike. Travelling to Lincoln and beyond was all a great mystery to me, and at thirteen, I thought it was time I struck out for myself, to broaden my horizons a bit. To me, London was at the other end of the world, and my family had never been away on holiday. Cleethorpes beach was our special treat, only a penny train ride away. We used to enjoy ourselves there, with Slater's Follies, the sand artists, Punch and Judy shows, Hancock's big amusement project and many other entertainments for youngsters. But I was getting a bit old for that now, or so I thought. A bike would take me out into the big world.

You could get a super bike brand new for three pounds – a Hercules Roadster. I was often seen putting my grubby face up at the cycle shop window. But I was just dreaming. In our family, even if I'd had three pounds to spare (which I didn't), there would have been more important things to spend it on. So, since I couldn't afford to buy a bike, I decided to make one.

Off I went round all the scrap yards, to see what I could find or beg. I was lucky enough to get hold of a frame, a saddle, two wheels and a pair of pedals. The wheels weren't up to much – I had to strip out all the old spokes, but before I did I worked out the formula for replacing them. It's complicated, because one side is different from the other. I managed to work it out though. Then I fitted new tapes inside the tyres and put fresh tubes in. After a while and quite a lot of hard work painting and assembling the parts, I succeeded in putting a decent machine together.

When Dad saw it, he was amazed. "You've made a good job of that lad," he told me. "It's better than one you could buy out of a shop window."

It was March, in fact my fourteenth birthday, in 1935, when I eventually left school, and by this time my old bike had totted up quite a few miles.

My father said, "Did you get your school report and reference from Mr. Potter?"

"Yes Dad, here it is."

He read them both with much enthusiasm. "They're very good lad. Now, I'm afraid there's going to be no holiday for you. You've a living to earn, and before you can do that you'll have to serve an apprenticeship. So you might as well start now."

So that was that. Fourteen years old, and as big as six pen'orth of coppers. Six o'clock in the morning. "Come on lad. Get up and have a swill under the tap. I'm not letting you laze about on street corners, getting into mischief. I'll take you down dock to see the gaffer, and see if he'll set you on. You might even make a fitter in time." In his own little way I knew he was proud of me, his eldest son.

"You'll get your arse kicked once or twice, but at least they'll make a man of you. You'll have to put a bit more meat on your bones, but they'll soon whip you into shape." After a few years I found out how right he was. He continued with further words of good advice. "Stand on your own two feet and you won't go far wrong. You'll have to mind your manners, and call the gaffer 'sir' at all times. And bloody well smarten yourself up. Here you are, shove this cap on your nut and come on. We'll get a mug of coffee at the cabin on the docks. It's a good walk but it'll wake you up." It was about a mile and a half.

When I stuffed the big cloth cap on my head, I could hardly see. But it was pouring with rain and it kept my head dry. I felt like a real man at last, but what a lot I had to learn.

Having reached the Fish Docks and had our mug of coffee, we turned in at the shipyard gates. "Take him to the gaffer's office Jack," the time-keeper yelled, "and don't worry lad, the gaffer won't eat you!"

Dad knocked at the office door, and I was scared stiff.

"Don't forget son, call him 'sir' and you'll be all right."

A big grey head poked round the door and shouted, "Come in sonny and take your cap off – that's if you can carry it!" (I thought, "Silly old sod".)

"Now then lad, you want to be an engineer, do you? You're not very big though, are you?" I was about four foot seven or eight.

"No sir," I said with excitement, "but I'm willing to work hard."

"We'll see sonny. If you're as good as your Dad, you'll do. But you'll have to work in the stores first, and do as you're told. Then after you've done two years, when you're sixteen, we'll see if we can make an apprentice fitter of you."

There was a big florid looking man in the office with him. "This is Mr. Bye, the outside foreman fitter. Take him down to the engineers' stores Herbert, and tell Bill Kelly to show him the ropes."

Down at the stores was a half door with a big counter on the top of it. My first job was to make a mug of tea for the stores boss, Bill, and his mate, Jim Bradley. Jim showed me where to boil the kettle, in the coppersmith's shop next door to the stores. The coppersmith's name was Fred Dowse, known to everyone as 'Klink' from his skill at forge brazing.

"Make one for yourself young Jack." Jim gave me three mugs, explaining that one in particular should be mine for my two years in the stores, and that I was to put my mark on it. He treated me like an equal then and thereafter. I liked his way of going on and knew that Bill, Jim and I were going to get on well together, and indeed we were to be great friends for many years.

Bill told me what my wage would be. "You'll get five and threepence a week, and your hours will be half-past-seven till five, Monday to Friday, and half-past-seven to twelve on Saturday. You get your wages on Saturday dinner at the time office hatch. You'll also be given a metal disc with your works number on, to be dropped in a basket after leaving the hatch. The firm holds three days in hand, so that means you'll be three days short this week.

"Be at the time office in good time, or you'll be sent home, and not be allowed to start till one o'clock. If you're early in the mornings, get the keys from the time office along with your time book, and you can come and unlock the stores."

Bloody hell. Did I feel important!

THE FORTY THIEVES

On the fish pontoon on a night without a moon
Only stars look down upon a silent town
And watch a trawler glide slowly in upon the tide
To where the lumpers stand for they've a catch to land

Well you've worked like hell and you've risked your life as well
And all the weeks at sea were worse than slavery
But if the trip's been good you don't mind the sweat & blood
Cos if the landing's fair then you'll pick up your share

> Chorus
> But you daren't even whisper
> You can only look
> And watch the lorries driven up
> And see the prime fish took
> Nobody talks about
> The old ghost train
> But the lorries & the fish
> Are never seen again

Now you weren't long at school but you're not a bloody fool
And all the prime fish sold is worth its weight in gold
And as you watch it go, man, it's robbery you know
But still you just look on until the ghost train's gone

There's a foolish few who've protested for the crew
They should have looked away, better had note to say
Now they'll not work again, though they're able trawlermen
You'll see them on the street, look how they drag their feet

> And you daren't even whisper …

Now the catch is ashore and the market's very poor
And the mate's in the galley reconciling his tally
And he's fifty kit short – fifty kit that wasn't caught
And wasn't spirited away before the light of day

There's more than one believes there's a band of forty thieves
Forty trawler owners and they'll have their bonus
And it's measured in lives and the tears of kids & wives
Who've seen their menfolk sail to perish in the gale

> And you daren't even whisper …

THE FORTY THIEVES

ONE MORE TRIP

When we let go on our latest trip, to me shipmates I did vow
"Oh, I'll never sign on with another ship, it's a shore job for me now"
But now we're steaming home, I know I love the open sea
With fifteen hundred kit below, it's one more trip for me

Chorus
One more trip to the northern seas, for to hear the seagulls wailin'
Where a wind is a calm and a gale is a breeze, then I've had me share of sailin'

There's a many fine night in me single days, on a drinkin' spree I've gone
With me pockets full and me thirst ablaze, and a pair of shoes that shone
But a restless life no more crave I, and a family man I'll be
And before I leave with a wistful sigh, it's one more trip for me

Well every time I'm on dry land, I declare I'll sail no more
For me pay don't stay long in me hand; I'll get a job on shore
But I know I'll miss the seagulls' cry, and I'll miss the roarin' sea
And it's hard to simply say "Goodbye" - it's one more trip for me

In the White Hart bar I've sat wi' me mates; such an 'andsome crew were we
And we'd drink a jar to the old lock gates, and our wedded wife, the sea
But the time has come for us to part, though it grieves me bitterly
And before my settled life I start, it's one more trip for me

Well, I can't go through my own whole life like a man without a home
I'm a stranger to me kids and wife; no more the seas I'll roam
Well it's homeward now we're steamin' fast; very soon we'll leave the sea
Ah but I can't make this trip my last - it's one more trip for me

ONE MORE TRIP

Verse: Whe-n we let go on our lat-est trip, to me ship-mates I did vow: "Oh, I'll

ne-ver sign on with an-oth-er ship. It's a shore job for me now." Bu-t

now we're steam-ing home, I know I love the op-en sea. Wi-th fif-teen hun-dred

kit be-low, it's one more trip for me. **Chorus:** One more trip to the north-ern seas, for to

hear the sea-gulls wail-in', where a wind is a calm and a gale is a breeze, then I've

had me share of sail-in'. There's a

JOHN EVARDSON

THE FISH DOCK RACES

On Friday afternoons at half-past-one, the schoolhouse gates all closes
The lads and lasses all troop out, droopy drawers and runny noses
Hundreds of kids are racing to the docks to get Dad's wages
And if you're late at the back o' the queue, you're standing there for ages

> Chorus
> The West Marsh kids are on the move; big parish boots make paces
> They're all let off on special leave to go to the Fish Dock Races

With yer hair stuck up & growin' like grass & your backside through yer trousers
Steppin' it out beside our lass with her drawers made from old blouses
There's women with kids hangin' on their skirts and bawlin' brats in prams
Down Charlton Street, Corporation Road, keepin' up wi' the clangin' trams

We've reached the wooden bridge, so old it never seemed safe to cross
The beams beneath as green as a toad, and all of 'em rotten with moss
We've crossed the Alexandra Dock and the Palace corner reached
Where the hands of the big Newmarket clock your eager eyes do seek

You'd see the old Newmarket Pub, running spittoon in the bar
The town's best beer you'd find in there, spit and sawdust (and your Pa)
But it's round the corner past the Palace Theatre now we're runnin'
The flea-pit Globe across the road, that you often used to get your fun in

Down from the top of Spiller's Mill a stone bulldog would face us
Victoria street School gates was locked on account of the Fish Dock Races
We're soon in Cleethorpe Road and past the Royal Hotel we're speedin'
Slip through the closin' railway gates and we'll gain the time we're needin'

We've passed the 'Railway' and the 'Coach', the crowd stopped by the gates
We laugh to see them push and shove, all cursin' their sad fates
But a copper stands at Riby Square, where Freeman Street we're meetin'
And lets a hundred bikes pass through, so it's with us they're competin'

So it's on we race, we're almost there – push on, we must keep goin'
We're at the office window now and they've hardly started queuin'
Then back by tram to dear old Mam, who's off her pledge to pay
To fetch Dad's suit back out of pawn – he's due to land today!

THE FISH DOCK RACES

On Friday afternoons at half-past-one, the school-house gates all closes. The lads and lasses all troop out, droopy drawers and runny noses. Hundreds of kids are racing to the Docks to get Dad's wages, And if you're late at the back o' the queue, you're standing there for ages.

Chorus:
The West Marsh kids are on the move, big parish boots make paces. They're all let off on special leave to go to the Fish Dock Races. With your

CHAPTER THREE

THE SAGA OF THE GIRL PAT

At this point I want to digress from the story of my own career, and touch upon that of a local man whose exploits captured the imagination not only of everyone in Grimsby and Cleethorpes, but of the whole nation.

If the happenings I'm about to relate were to take place today, they would no doubt be labelled a 'hi-jack' by the press. Though in this case the only 'hostages' were the unfortunate rogues who helped to carry out their misguided leader's ill-fated plan.

During the course of their adventure the name of their little trawler was on everyone's lips, and their exploits made newspaper headlines, bringing the crew, their boat and the port of Grimsby into the national limelight. This was how it happened.

During my time in Consol's engineers' stores, the port acquired a new small motor diesel trawler, a revolutionary prototype of seine net trawlers of the future. The year was 1935. She had been named 'The Girl Pat', and her proud owners needed a competent skipper and crew to put her through her paces on her maiden trip.

There lived in the town an adventurous seaman of the time called George Orsborne, or 'Dod' as he was known as a skipper, a good trawlerman and a skilled navigator. Well qualified to master the vessel, he was duly contracted by the owners. They expected him to prove the worth of their sturdy little ship as a North Sea trawler. They could never have guessed just how well 'Dod' was to test the boat's sea-worthiness and endurance.

For Skipper Orsborne there was something very special about the trip he was about to make. He insisted upon personally handpicking his crew, each one of whom had sworn to be faithful to his secret cause. He appointed his brother, Jim, as second-in-command. In fact, only these two knew for certain their intended destination.

To allay the suspicions of the owners, 'Dod' had not dared give a hint of his true intention. An unusual chandler's order might raise a few eyebrows in the owners' offices. So he hadn't been able to make full provision, obtain proper charts or make due allowance for anything that might go wrong on such an ambitious voyage as he had in mind. Though 'The Girl Pat' was a sound vessel, and her crew tough and experienced, they were North Sea bred, and totally unprepared for the tropical conditions they were about to face.

For the incredible truth was that Jim Orsborne had acquired (how I can't tell) an old pirate's chart of buried treasure, which it appeared lay somewhere in the archipelago of islands in the notorious Carlsberg Ridge of the Indian Ocean, the Seychelles. This was to be their goal.

Ironically they set out from Grimsby on Monday, 1st April. The boat headed into the Humber shipping lanes and made full speed ahead for the North Sea, then starboard on a southbound heading. Her first port of call would be Dover. Having brought no charts for the journey, Dod's brother went ashore in the small boat and bought a school atlas from a stationer's shop in the town. From there they shaped their course for Calais.

At this stage the crew was jubilant. They spliced the mainbrace, and drank to the success of their venture. From Calais they headed for Portugal, never imagining what fearsome times lay ahead.

That night as they entered the Bay of Biscay, engines throbbing and sails well set, the glass started to drop and they ran into heavy seas. They were subjected to thunder and lightning and waves like mountains, which tossed the little ship about like a cork in a bucket. The engine developed a fault and the boat drifted helplessly in a cauldron of water whipped up by gales and driving rain.

How could they survive? But the courageous skipper lashed himself to the wheel and managed to maintain control, driven on by his fabulous dream and tremendous bravery, while his brother tried in vain to repair the stricken engine. After three days drifting at last the weather subsided. Under sail alone they steered for their nearest landfall.

By now they were badly in need of supplies, food, fresh water and of course repairs to the engine. Sailing to Corubion by Cape Finisterre, by dubious methods they were able to raise some money for the necessary work but during their stay of fifteen days were unable to commission anyone to carry out the job. So once more they set out under sail.

Nine blistering days and languishing nights at sea took them to the Spanish African port of Rio-de-Oro, where they arrived exhausted and scorched by the pitiless sun. Their spirits lifted slightly at this glimpse of civilisation, though not really knowing what to expect, they dropped anchor and launched the smallboat.

Having rowed half way ashore, they could make out what seemed to be a reception committee waving to them. Getting closer they began to see more clearly that the impending reception was to be far from friendly. For the party on the bank comprised the most vicious tribe of hostile Arabs anyone could wish to meet, armed to the teeth with guns and knives!

The hapless travellers turned around and, despite their weakness, made it back to The Girl Pat hell for leather, and set sail again without delay.

Surely their run of bad luck must end soon. For a while it seemed that it would. Dod set his course for Cape Bianco and managed to reach the port. Here he was able to obtain food from the friendly natives. However having left no night watch aboard while they took their shore leave, they returned to find their gear had been ransacked. An understanding Spaniard offered his services to pilot them into Etienne. But with no funds to pay him with, they had to put out the next morning with neither pilot nor charts for their southbound journey.

Not far off Etienne the 'Lass' got grounded on a sandbank. After three days in distress they were able to re-float her on the high tide. But after only a few hours they beached her again. Close to despair they nearly gave up hope. She had a forty degree list and her starboard rail was actually under water. To cap it all a fierce gale was now starting to blow, adding to their peril. With the nearest safe landfall forty miles off they were at a loss to know what to do, except pray, which one or two of them actually did.

Suddenly the wind dropped and the ship slowly slid off the shoal water and into a floating position. After a few hours of pumping out they gained an even keel into deep water. Famished and worn out, Dod made for Dakar. There he might be able to obtain food and water, and perhaps even fuel oil and get the engine restored.

What was to have been a short North Sea maiden voyage had developed into a macabre cruise extending into months, and naturally the folks at home were wondering what had become of the Girl Pat's crew. Everyone suspected there was mischief afoot, but the press was playing up the suspense and excitement.

Although the adventure had become a pathetic situation, Grimsby was revelling in the fame and interest being created by the local craft and her crew. Their families waited every day for weeks on end at the docks entrance, hoping to see the Girl come through the lock gates. But it was a hopeless and heartbreaking drama for the worried wives and children. I used to see them on the corner every day, and some of the wives appeared to age a great deal over those few weeks. Of course there was no weekly pay to collect, so they were forced to rely on charity to keep their children fed in the meantime.

Dod must have realised by now that the world was looking for them, and that after all these weeks there must be a huge search going on for the vessel. So he got one of the crew to paint out the ship's name before they entered Dakar, and re-christened her 'Kia-Ora'.

When they docked at Dakar, Dod gave his name as Skipper George Black, destination Cape Town. He used all his charm and powers of persuasion to obtain stores and get the engine repaired, with new injectors, exhaust and inlet valves being fitted by the next morning. All this without having the means to pay. Dod insisted that he test the engine before settling up, and foolishly the chandlers agreed.

Heading out to sea slowly at first, when just out of sight he opened her up to full speed. The merchants and ship's agents saw no more of them or their money. But it wasn't long before they were able to put two and two together. Immediately the news flashed around the world. The Girl Pat had been found at last.

It was the beginning of the end. Eventually, and inevitably, they were arrested just off Georgetown, British Guiana, but only after a long hard chase by the gunboat that sighted them.

The boat and crew were escorted back to England for trial, but were greeted on their arrival by a welcoming hoard of admiring sightseers. They had been at sea for fourteen weeks, and their bold but foolhardy escapade had earned them a kind of popular respect – in fact they were public heroes.

However the fact remained that the law had been broken. George and Jim stood trial for piracy at the Old Bailey, and got off rather lightly. Eighteen months and twelve months hard labour respectively was their punishment.

As for the treasure, as far as I know it could still be in the Seychelles somewhere, waiting to be found. But one thing is for certain. Whoever sets out to find it, even if they're armed with more sophisticated navigation aids than a child's school atlas, will need at least as much daring, courage and determination as the remarkable George 'Dod' Orsborne.

JOHN EVARDSON

THE GIRL PAT

In the Humber bar on a freezing night rear end of thirty-five
I was brim full of ale far away from the gale and the happiest man alive
For the bold George Orsborne was raising a crew and offering wealth and fame
On a venturous trip in a brand new ship and The Girl Pat was her name

> Chorus
> They sailed away on All Fools' Day; their needs were small and few
> A penny school atlas, a brand new boat, and a good stout Grimsby crew

She was built to fish the North Sea coast, her owner's joy and pride
Ah but no herring shoal was to be our goal as we sailed on the morning tide
For the Orsborne brothers had heard of gold, long buried in foreign parts
Its whereabouts known to those two alone, so they'd not enquired for charts

It was south to Dover first we struck, then the Channel we swiftly sailed
Then around from Calais to the Bay of Biscay where, alas, our engines failed
So by canvas alone we steered for Spain and landed at Cape Finisterre
Where we found some relief from tinned corn beef but the engines couldn't repair

So for fifteen days 'neath a blistering sky in murderous heat sailed we
And we feared under sail that our quest must fail in that cruel Atlantic sea
And wherever we tried for repairs or supplies, small welcome there we found
Till the Girl struck sand forty mile from land, high and dry off Etienne Sound

Well, the wind soon blew an almighty gale and we thought our end was due
All starved and afraid, we knelt and prayed, though a tough hard North Sea crew
Three terrible days we waited in dread till she floated off that bar
With a limp and a list, knowing well we'd be missed, we slipped into Dakar

To obtain repairs, supplies and fuel, our skipper disguised his name
For in every port the Girl Pat was sought and he'd have to conceal her fame
He vowed he'd settle before we sailed, and the foolish merchants agreed
To an engine trial, but after a mile, we made for sea at full speed

Now the news flashed round the globe to say the Girl Pat had been found
To the west we sailed wi' the world on our trail till we saw South American ground
But a Georgetown gunboat was lying in wait, then oh! How we gave them a show!
What a furious race as their boat gave chase, till at length they took us in tow

When the crew got back to Grimsby Town we'd a heroes' welcome there
For we'd sailed her well through the gates of hell, and o' trouble we'd had our share
But the doughty Orsbornes were sent for trial, and got eighteen and twelve
    months' hard
For taking and stealing the best little boat to come out of an English yard

THE GIRL PAT

Verse:
In the Hum-ber bar on a free-zing night, rear end of thir-ty - five, I was

brim-full of ale, far a - way from the gale and the hap-pi-est man a - live. For the

bold George Ors-borne was rais-ing a crew and off-er-ing wealth and fame, On a

ven-tur-ous trip in a brand-new ship and The Girl Pat wa-s her name.

Chorus:
They sailed a-

- way on All Fool's Day, their needs were small and few: A pen-ny school at-las, a

brand-new boat and a good stout Gri-ms-by crew. She was

WHERE THE SEA MEETS THE LAND

Where the sea meets the sky, that's your Daddy's world now
Where the wind has no mercy nor gives up its row
Below the horizon, far from the sea strand
Steaming hard for the cold northern seas of Iceland

<u>Chorus</u>
And when Daddy returns
We'll be here, where the sea meets the land

When we're snug in our beds on a wintry black night
There are fishermen out where the storm's at its height
Where cold is a word that we can't understand
There's no wonder they paint the town red when they finally land

When they're fishing, they work for two-thirds of the day
It's a life without romance whatever they say
Smashing ice off the cables, as thick as your hand
For the cruel north will sink you if ever it can

I was young when we wed, and your Daddy was too
For the sea and the wind make a man out of you
We were glad of a bai'n even though you weren't planned
Now your Dad's working hard till they make him third hand

Sometimes on the Pontoon you'll see children and wives
With a smile for the men who've been risking their lives
Farewell to three weeks of the skipper's command
It's a joy to be home with your feet on dry land!

WHERE THE SEA MEETS THE LAND

Verse:
Where the sea meets the sky, that's your Dad-dy's world now, Where the wind has no

mer-cy, nor gives up its row; Be-low the hor - i-zon, far from the sea strand.

Steam-ing hard for the cold north-ern seas of Ice - land.

Chorus:
And when

Dad-dy re - turns, we'll be here where the sea meets the land. When we're

SIX TILL TWO

Chorus
Morning shift, six till two
I feel cold, how about you?
Me face is red and me legs are blue
In me wellies and me turban on the six till two

February morning, couldn't be worse
You leave your warm bed and you don't half curse
You creep out the house, you make no fuss
Then you're running like a greyhound for the early bus

Six o'clock start, the girls file past
Take your card to the clock – I'm sure it's fast
A smile for the night shift and they're soon gone
But the fish finger line goes on and on

You chatter to Mabel, you chatter to Elaine
Natterin's the only thing to keep you sane
You laugh and you gasp at the gossip that's told
Then suddenly it's quiet and it ain't half cold

Look out, here's the red hat, to stand and smirk
And look down her nose at the ones who work
She thinks she's a queen in her chargehand's hat
But when she's gone we've better names for her than that

We don't get low, though we hate this shift
It's pay day soon and it's not to be sniffed
We give 'em our time and they give us our due
But no-one's here for pleasure on the six till two

When two o'clock comes you're jiggered as a rule
But you hurry to the shops before the kids leave school
Your one consolation's your summer holiday
You'll never get to Butlin's on your old man's pay

SIX TILL TWO

Chorus:
Morn-ing shift, six till two, I feel cold, how a-bout you? Me face is red and me

legs are blue In me wel-lies and me tur-ban on the six till two.

Verse:
Feb-ru-ar-y morn-ing,

could-n't be worse; You leave your warm bed and you don't half curse. You

creep out the house, you make no fuss, Then you're runn-ing like a grey-hound for the

ear-ly bus.

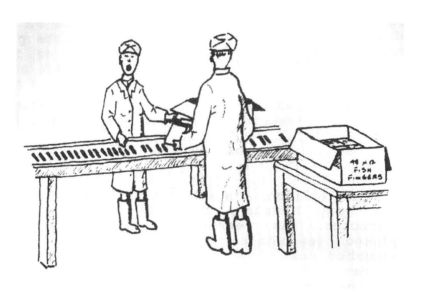

SEA BIRD

CHAPTER FOUR

OF RATS AND MEN

Having begun my working life with great enthusiasm, I commenced to learn as much as I could about the tools and spares kept in the stores. Although it would be two whole years before I could get a chance at an apprenticeship, this humble job was at least a beginning, and I was determined to make the most of it. I soon found that it could offer a bit of variety too. For apart from the usual store-keeping duties, it appeared that there were one or two other extra little chores for a trainee apprentice.

For one thing, the time books had to be carried down to the main office once a week in a big canvas bag. Now as you know, I was no heavyweight, nor could you say that I was tall – in fact, while serving at the stores counter I used to have to stand on a wooden box! Later on, continuous hard graft would improve my stature and physique, but to the little short-arse that I was then, that pile of books seemed enormous. I thought, "These must weigh a bloody ton!" Yet somehow I managed the journey, and before long that weekly task began to call for less and less effort.

Another little job concerned the firm's owner, Sir John Marsden, who lived on a big estate called Panton Hall. He used to be chauffeur-driven to the docks, then he would walk down to the office for his board meeting. The usual procedure was to walk about a yard behind the 'great man', carrying his case to the office. He was always smoking a big cigar – you know, about the size that Churchill smoked. The perk of the job was to be able to rescue his four-inch butt, to be enjoyed later at my leisure.

After two years in the stores I knew every nut, bolt, screw, jointing compound, tool and engine casting that ever was used on a steam trawler.

Bill came out of his office one day and said to me, "Come here young Jack. Arthur Gidley the gaffer wants to see you in his office. Don't worry – I've put in a good word for you."

Trembling I went to Mr. Gidley's office, quietly knocked and waited. "Come in sonny," he boomed. I went in. "And shut the door." As I did so I could see that he was leaning over some drawings on his desk. There was a scale model of a trawler in a glass case in the window.

"See that ship there?" he asked. "We have over a hundred of those fishing all over the northern hemisphere – North Sea, Dogger Bank, Rockall, Faroes, Greenland, White Sea, Iceland, Grand Banks and Newfoundland, to mention just a few.

"We have some good young and old tradesmen in this firm, I'm proud to say, and we need the best that money can buy to keep the finest fishing fleet in Britain up to scratch.

"After the glowing report I've had from Bill Kelly, I've decided to take you on as an apprentice engineering fitter. The main engines are all triple expansion reciprocating engines, and they need precise and exact maintenance. Don't ever let me down or I'll have your guts for garters. And remember – all those trawler crews' lives are in your hands."

He paused, but I was too excited to say anything, and I was nearly quaking under the weight of all this sudden responsibility!

I was glad when Mr. Gidley brought the audience to an end. "That's all then sonny. Report to the acting shop foreman Mr. Howse in the fitting shop in the morning."

As I walked out of his office, I thought, "Thank God that's over!"

So the following day I reported to my new place of work. The shop foreman at that time was Harry Burrell, but he was off work seriously ill. He was being deputised by the shop chargehand, one of the most pleasant men I have ever met. His name was Mr. Howse, or (as he told me straight away) to all his mates, 'Les' – and he was known as 'Les' to all and sundry. Just a few weeks later he was to become the official foreman when poor old Harry Burrell passed away.

Les held his hand out and said, "Welcome to the fold young Jack. I hope you'll make the grade, and if you take notice of the fitters in here you won't go far wrong."

"Yes Mr. Howse, I will," I replied, acting all shy and respectful, and trying to make a good impression.

"Keep your eyes and ears open and you'll soon get the idea. But first and foremost do as you're told."

Next he introduced me to all the fitters, turners and machinists one by one. He then showed me my own bench, which was equipped with a vice so old it would have made a prize exhibit in the British Museum. (After a few weeks I was able to acquire a new one.)

The tool drawer contained files of all shapes and sizes. I soon found out that the three-quarter file was the most useful one in the set. I said to one of the fitters, "Don't I need some more tools mister?"

"You've no need to call me 'mister' young Jack. My name is Bill Ward; just call me 'Bill' and we'll get on flipping fine." I discovered later that Bill was a Methodist lay preacher at the George Street Mission in Cleethorpes. A fine man and a good fitter, he never swore, but used other adjectives when he needed to vent his feelings.

He put me on the right track by telling me what spanners I would need from the stores. "These are all open-jawed spanners, all Whitworth sizes, from three-eighths of an inch. Ask Les for an order to take to the stores. You'll also want a two pound hammer and shaft."

After thanking Bill, I eventually got all my spanners in the bench drawer. The hammer and shaft were still on my bench, when the senior apprentice came up behind me and said, "Hello young Jack, I'm Arthur Green. You want to take your hammer and shaft into the carpenters' shop and get it properly shafted. But before you do, go and get your shaft exchanged for a straight-grained one." I thanked Arthur for his advice, and was pleased to have made another friend.

I spent a few months on the bench and then went my rounds on the different machines, finishing up on the lathe. It was an old machine, only used by the apprentices, and appropriately named 'Leaping Lena' by the lads because of its erratic behaviour. The machines were all belt-driven, with counter-shafting and belts for each lathe, drilling machine, etcetera. The main shafting was run from a mains-driven motor near the shop front sliding door.

One of the tasks we four apprentices performed was to bore and turn brass bushes and pins for gallows rollers, for the trawl-lifting gear. The gallows was a U-shaped structure, made from six-inch H-iron, with big steel rollers top and bottom fitted port and starboard, fore and aft, used for lifting the heavy wire warps and nets.

I fell for all the practical jokes the youngest apprentice always has to suffer, like being sent to the stores for a 'long stand' and waiting half an hour before twigging it, or going into the blacksmiths' shop for a 'bag of blast'. It was always the youngest apprentice's job to run the errands for the men, for nuts and bolts, jointing and cotton waste and the like from the stores. It was also the custom to run all the other errands, like fetching fags, tobacco and daily papers.

Another chore that must not be forgotten was the Friday morning trip for the fish and chip dinners, after which the lad used to receive a collective tip of about two bob, a useful amount to us in those days. The fish and chips, a 'tuppenny and a pen'orth', as you can work out cost threepence, and consisted of a large piece of haddock, cod, skate or plaice and chips, with plenty of vinegar and salt on. I would fetch about twelve portions and they always made a good meal.

Some of the blokes brought their own packing up, or dinners in containers to heat up in the oven, a makeshift one built on top of the large slow combustion stoves that were cluttered about the shop to keep the machinery running smoothly in the winter.

Well, one man 'Nobby' Clark asked me to put his dinner in the oven as he was working outside on a ship. I put his container in at about a quarter to twelve.

When he arrived in the shop at twelve he said to me, "Did you put my dinner in to warm up Jack?"

"It's over there on the stove Nobby," I said, pointing. He took the tin and sat down to enjoy a good dinner, only to find that his wife had packed him up fruit jelly and custard, now a steaming hot mush! He threw it across the shop yelling, "Why didn't she tell me?" (It seems he was in the doghouse for being on the booze the night before.) "Fetch me some fish and chips will you please Jack? I'll waltz her round when I get home!"

Working on the bench one day, using my hammer and chisel, I hit my thumb and it split open in three places like a ripe tomato. It healed up after a week or two, but it was bloody agony at the time and I made sure I never hit my hand again. (I am over sixty now and still carry the scars.)

The secret of using a hammer and cold chisel is not to watch the top of your chisel, but to keep your eye on the cutting edge. I used to show my protégés in later years a simple method I'd learned from older apprentices.

Make a chalk dot in the middle of the solid bench. Place the index finger of your left hand about two inches from the dot and move it from left to right, then right to left, while striking the dot with the hammer, always keeping your eyes on the dot. After a while, with confidence gained, you can quicken the movement and cover the chalk spot with every stroke. The proper use of a hammer is an art, holding it as far up the shaft as feels comfortable, thereby getting the most force applied with the minimum effort.

The fitting shop work was hard, or so I thought, but there were harder times to come. Meanwhile there was a little fun thrown in of our own making.

We used to have a toilet comprising a piece of wood over a channel with four holes in appropriate positions, partitioned off with wooden walls on each side of the holes, and half door fronts. At each end was a proper flush toilet, to be used only by the foremen. These were separated from the rest by a brick wall, and to flush the men's toilets, someone had to flush the foremen's, and the water would rush straight through and out the other end. You can imagine how antiquated the building was, and it was an open invitation to us lads to have a bit of a lark.

As you must know, in those times the habit of having a fag at work was strictly forbidden, so the toilets were the only place for the men to have a crafty smoke and make their racing selections.

We found some stubs of tallow candles and stuck each one to a piece of wood. Sneaking into one of the foremen's cubicles, we waited until the men's thrones were all occupied, placed the 'fireships' in the channel and lit the candles. Then we pulled the chain to float them down one by one, and got out of the way pretty smartish.

What a commotion! All the doors came flying open and out flew our victims, stuffing their papers up their jumpers, and at the same time trying to pull their pants up, with faces as red as beetroots and uttering such colourful phrases! If they'd caught us we'd have been shot at dawn, but we survived to think up other pranks.

There was another instance involving the tinsmiths' shop foreman, 'Sparrow Jack', so-called because of his small stature and peculiar walk. His shop labourer Tommy Slack used to clean the windows regularly. This particular day the apprentice tinsmiths were playing about and accidentally broke Sparrow's office window, and the little foreman would be back at any moment.

Well, the lads were in a panic, but not our Tommy. "Leave it to me lads, and he'll never know the difference."

So he picked all the old glass out and cleaned the place up, then carried on cleaning the office windows just as Jack walked in, and pretended to clean the non-existent pane as well. As Jack sat down in his chair, Tommy grinned, "There you are boss, all ship-shape and Bristol fashion. Should I mek you a cup of tea?"

Sparrow beamed approval. "Bloody hell, you're a marvel Tom. And look at this office, it sparkles – it looks the brightest and smartest in the yard, and that's sayin' summat. Wish the old lass knew your secret."

While he spoke he put his hand up to the door 'window' and of course it went right through. "Some joker's pinched the bloody window Tom! Go and fetch Percy Marris the plumber foreman to put a new one in."

As you can gather a trawler firm was very self-reliant in those days. We even made our own tins and pans. But the various skills of the many resourceful tradesmen employed by Consolidated Fisheries went beyond the bounds of engineering.

There was a fitter called Harry Greenbury, a king among fitters, in fact a very clever man by all standards. He knew a lot of short cuts to solving many practical problems. Now old Sparrow Jack, a Meggie (born in Cleethorpes), was plagued with rats in his back garden, and decided to ask Harry if he knew a quick solution to his predicament. His dear wife was terrified of them and was forever telling him what a useless old sod he was, so he approached Harry, cap in hand, and told him of his plight.

"Well, look here Jack," said Harry, "be it on your own head, but I'll tell you of a method that's been well tried, with a hundred per cent success. Mind you, being a man of principle as I know you are, it's probably beyond your ethics to do it."

"What do you mean Harry?" enquired Jack.

"Well, it means you pinching some calcium carbide."

"I can soon do that Harry," he said, full of excitement. (Though if he'd known of anyone else stealing from the firm, Sparrow would have got him the sack straight away.)

"All right then," the expert continued. "You must know that carbide is a very volatile substance under certain conditions, so for God's sake don't fool around with it. Now what you should do is go round your back garden and fill all the holes in you can see, with just one exception – that is, the biggest one. When all the others are filled in, drop some carbide down the last hole, then pour some water down and wait for five minutes."

"Yes Harry, then what?" urged Jack, all eager to learn the great secret.

"Apply a lighted match, then stand well back." The lesson had ended. This was on a Saturday afternoon.

Monday morning came, and Sparrow Jack was on the warpath. He ran into the fitting shop shouting, "Where's that bloody Greenbury?"

"Here I am Sparrow," chuckled Harry. "What's the matter – it didn't go wrong did it? I told you to be careful."

"Careful? Careful?" raved Jack. "How bloody careful can you be?"

"Sit down and tell us what happened then," grinned Harry, calm and patient as ever.

"Well, I did what you told me," said Jack. "I waited five minutes, then threw a lighted match in the hole. There was such an unholy rumble, then a deafening explosion, and the bloody lavatory shot straight across the back yard, carrying the closet door with it! It's going to cost me a fortune. Never again. Never again," he moaned, holding his head in his hands.

By now Harry was laughing fit to drop. "Your missus wasn't on the throne was she Jack? And anyway, you've got rid of the rats, they'll not be back – the whole rat population of Cleethorpes will steer clear of you now!"

Sparrow Jack waddled away, muttering, "My old lass is giving me hell. My life won't be worth living from now on."

After a full year in the fitting shop, Les the foreman called me into his office one afternoon and said it was time for me to work outside on the ships. I would be starting the next morning, and must stand in line with the outside fitters to get my orders from Herbert Bye, the outside foreman. (He was known as 'Checker' because of his driving methods.) I felt very excited to be starting work on the ships that put the 'Great' into 'Great Grimsby'. By this time I'd grown a bit and had become more thick set and very muscular. I was never afraid of hard work, in fact I revelled in it.

I was first put with an old fitter called Harry Rowston, a nice old man in his early sixties, and a very good practical fitter. He was a type I would describe now as a 'rule of thumb' fitter, who always double-checked a job before he left it. We got on real well, old Harry and I, and I can still picture him today after all these years. A characteristic of his, when he'd finished a job, was to hitch up his truss, rub his hands over his nose, and say to me, "Thanks pal - that'll catch haddocks!"

It was 1938, and they were laying up ships at Winnipeg from all over the Fish Docks, and a firm called Markham-Cook's had just taken delivery of some German trawlers, registered out of London to pay off part of the war debt. These were the original 'Northern' boats, and Markham-Cook's, Letten's and one or two more local firms joined forces, built some big new offices and called their new firm 'Northern Trawlers Limited'.

Well, my eccentric old mate Harry took sick and passed away, God rest his soul. Then I teamed up with a fitter called Fred Bealy, and he said that it was the best day's work he'd ever done when he'd asked for me. The feeling of respect was mutual. You see, although Fred was a lot older than me and an exceptional tradesman, we also became great comrades.

Generally the job was a bit rough for a time, but the interest overruled the hard work, so I soon got used to it and could muck in with the best of them, and I began to get really tough and hardy. The life suited me. I was strong and as fit as a fiddle.

We were expected to work in all the worst conditions, temperatures hot and cold, rain and snow. There was little in the way of protective clothing in those days. One minute we'd be working in the blistering heat of an engine room with boilers running at a hundred degrees or more, then you'd find us up on deck in freezing weather, still wet through, with the sweat drying cold on us. We had no choice than to be fit and strong. Some of us would pay the price though, when in later life the extremes we had to face as young men left us with weakened constitutions, and old before our time.

Still it was good to be able to work hard and do your bit, in spite of the hardships. And of course, there were always odd bits of excitement or amusing incidents to divert your attention from the rigours of a fitter's life.

I'll never forget the time we were taking a big piston valve cylinder off an arctic winch, weighing about half a ton, to fit a new one. The ship in question was berthed on the northeast side of the Iceland jetty, commonly known as 'Pneumonia', owing to the fact that it always caught the freezing weather. It was located where the old floating dry dock used to be. Well, we'd managed to get the old cylinder ashore by manpower, using the hand windlass and the for'ard jiltson wire. We now had to get the new one back the same way, but in reverse order.

We shackled the replacement, which also weighed half a ton, to a three-inch check rope, passing this through a pulley on the side of the bridge casing. This 'fair lead' acted as a check for the cylinder as it was lifted by the jiltson wire, which was fed through another pulley on the top of the mast. Now as it had to be lifted a few inches clear of the jetty, the idea was to raise it by manpower with a turn around a shore bollard.

As luck would have it, we were at the end of the Pontoon, close to where the fish train express trucks were being loaded up. So, having got the cylinder lifted and swung inboard, a bright spark decided (can you guess?) to make the jiltson wire fast to the buffer on the end of the guard's van, while the fitters got the cylinder ready to be lifted into position.

Well of course, 'Sod's Law' came into its own. That is – the worst possible thing that can happen will happen. Which it did. Without any warning whatsoever, the fish train started off, bound for markets in London and all points south.

Immediately the cylinder started to ascend the mast like a cotton bobbin, and panic stations were put into operation. Herbert Bye had to think and act quickly. He jumped on his bike, his legs going up and down like piston rods at full speed to stop the train, and get it to back up. Although he was no spring chicken, he must have broken all known records, for he just managed to catch the driver's attention in time. The train screeched to a halt, with the cylinder only a split second away from causing untold damage and probably injury into the bargain.

There were sighs of relief all round, and we were soon able to winch the cylinder into position. However, although actual damage had been averted, there were financial repercussions against the firm, for stopping a special train owned by the London and North Eastern Railway on their own property.

(The docks and surrounding area at that time all belonged to the then privately-owned railway companies.)

I liked and enjoyed my job as a steam engine fitter. Though it didn't leave much time for the ordinary pleasures of life, it was really a labour of love. Don't get me wrong, it was a very hard and exacting job, but the ultimate reward of our work was to see our engines run after a complete overhaul – they were like poetry in motion. I firmly believe there is not, nor ever will be, in any shape or form on sea or land, any other source of motive power comparable to the steam engine, when well nursed and lovingly maintained.

And I could enjoy my work even more when I turned eighteen, because now the law allowed me to work unlimited overtime. I would not throw this opportunity away, as it would enable me to increase the small contributions I made towards my keep at home.

One night Fred and I had been working late, to finish off a major overhaul we'd been doing on the main engines of one of the big Iceland trawlers, which was lying head-on at the North Wall, and due to sail on the next tide. She bore the name 'Huddersfield Town' (nearly all the firm's Arctic trawlers being named after first division football teams).

It was a bad winter's night in March 1939. I'll always remember it as long as I live.

Fred gave me his book to put in the time office, and said he was going home over the Humber Street bridge. That just left George Cribb, the most experienced fitter's labourer in existence, and yours truly. George was as good as any average fitter, and another great friend of mine, who for a change had been an addition to our little team for a few weeks now, and had worked very hard. He slung the greasy old tool bag over his shoulder and said, "Come on young Jack, let's get going. It's well gone eleven."

We were two huddled figures descending the stern ladder of the trawler onto the wet concrete of the North Wall. The wind howled through the riggings of the ranks of ships at berth, and the horizontal drive of the sleet in the force nine gale seemed to tear our faces to ribbons. Through heavy cloud there was only intermittent moonlight to guide our way homewards.

I yelled through the screaming storm, "Which way shall we go George? I'm bloody well tired out, and it's just coming up to midnight!" The lockpit island clock had an illuminated face, and I could just make out the time.

"Right young Jack," answered George. "We'll take the short cut, across the lockpit!"

We crossed the lock in the buttressing sleet, and turned left at the old herring slip, into Fish Dock Road. Eerily, the wind died down to a breeze, and the sleet and rain petered out. Only the scraping of our hobnailed boots on the wet granite cobbles echoed back in the darkness of that unearthly night.

George stopped, and signalled me to do likewise. "Wait here a minute," he whispered. "Can you hear or smell owt?" I couldn't, but from his tone I knew something was wrong.

There was now an absolute hush in the cold night air, and a chill ran down my spine. I could actually feel the colour draining from my face as George, who didn't scare easily, backed into a shop doorway, as though trying to make his body merge with the woodwork. Urgently he beckoned, "Come on young Jack, get in here quick. You're going to see the most terrifying sight you've ever seen in your life!"

We hunched ourselves together, getting as close up to that doorway as was humanly possible, and though a bitterly cold night, the sweat was beading on our brows. Then I caught that foul smell on the wind, and in the blackness could be heard the thumping of hundreds of padded feet. There was no doubt about it. Both the smell and the sound were getting nearer every second. I was uttering a silent prayer for our deliverance, and wishing we'd gone the long way round instead.

"For God's sake keep still and don't move a muscle!" urged George. "We might be all right if we keep dead still!"

We saw it then, a big black shape with sharp, beady eyes, bounding along the cobbled road towards us. It was a giant, easily the most enormous rat I'd ever seen – and I'd seen quite a few on board the ships. This one was as big as a large cat, obviously a king among rats, and without doubt able to rip out the throat of any luckless person who happened to cross its path.

And if this was the king, we hadn't long to wait for the retinue.

For now came the holocaust. Thousands of rats, of all shapes and sizes, quickly filled the road and paths, in an apparent frenzy to follow their leader. We cringed as they even ran over our boots to get past. Desperately they surged onwards. Just as desperately we cowered in the doorway, praying we wouldn't be noticed, and fearing for our lives. I'd never felt so helpless – there was nothing to do but to remain motionless and watch the sickening spectacle as the detestable hoard went past us.

As for the noise, well, the earlier screaming of the gale was as nothing compared to the sound we now had to endure. The chattering and screeching of those creatures was like the sound of a night scene in a tropical forest, only increased a thousand times. It seemed to me that all the noise in the world was contained in that narrow street at that moment. And there was no question of muffling the sound by putting our hands over our ears. I thought my eardrums would burst, but knew I must endure the deafening row, remain still, and wait, and hope.

All through this ordeal, as if that wasn't enough, we had to try and breathe – an almost impossible task, since the overwhelming stench was all but unbearable. It was as if they had brought with them every obnoxious smell that they had collected from all the nasty, putrid, slimy, stinking places they'd ever been.

After what seemed an age, the seething mass of hellish vermin had gone, and we heaved sighs of relief at the peace and tranquillity that now settled over the area. With a shudder we silently left the docks and completed our trek homewards. In the distance we could just see the rat population split into two groups, one turning into part of the Royal Dock, and the remainder going left onto the fish area of the Iceland jetty. But I am sure that the big leading rat carried straight on over the Docks Railway Crossing, and into the old town.

TO THE TRADES

<u>Chorus</u>
Let's drink to the trades that keep the trawlers sailin'
The men and women on the shore who serve the lads at sea
The boiler suit brigade – you'll never find 'em failin'
So another round of ale in and we'll drink to the trades!

There's blacksmiths, there's tinsmiths, there's coppersmiths an' all
There's f-f-frozen fitters on the flippin' cold North Wall
There's boilermakers, shipwrights, rivetters, platers too
So tradesmen all we'll raise a glass to you!

You'll find us after work each night in any dockside pub
A pint or two before we shuffle home to have our grub
To swap a yarn with trawlermen and tradesmen at the bar
All proud when we remember who we are

The braiders work at home for pennies mekkin' up the nets
Workin' hard as wives as well while payin' off the debts
There's sailmakers and riggers, the men who mind the store
And the lads who mek the tea and sweep the floor

Now come all you apprentice lads – you've got a lot to learn
How tradesmen give their sweat and blood for the pittance that they earn
Though the battle for a decent livin' won't be easy won
There's the satisfaction of a job well done

There's many more who do their bit – our lab'rers and our mates
The taxi drivers and the lockpitmen who mind the gates
The barmaids and the bookie's clerks, the blokes who cut our hair
And the naughty girls who stand at Riby Square!

TO THE TRADES

Chorus:
Let's drink to the trades that keep the trawl-ers sail-in', the men and wom-en on the shore who serve the lads at sea. The boil-er suit brig - ade, you'll nev-er find 'em fail-in' So an-oth-er round of ale in and we'll drink to the trades.

Verse:
There's black-smiths, there's tin-smiths, there's cop-per-smiths an' all. There's f - f - fro-zen fit-ters on the flip-pin' cold North Wall. There's boil-er mak-ers, ship-wrights, riv-et-ers, pla-ters too. So trades-men all we'll raise a glass to you! Let's

THE GRAND OLD LADIES

In the Albion one chilly evenin' I was warmin' meself by the fire
When I spied in the corner an old fisherman who I thought I'd engage to enquire:
If I stood him a pint could he tell me any trips he'd a mind to recall?
Well he gave me a wink, then he parked his drink, sayin': Aye lad - I've sailed wi' 'em all

> Chorus
> We called 'em the Grand Old Ladies
> That took us to the Arctic Grounds
> Here's a tribute paid to the ships that made
> The Trawlin' Trade go round
> The Trawlin' Trade go round

Well he'd signed on wi' Bannister's & Boston's, then wi' Moody's & Mudd's & Macrill's
Aye & Cooks & Kelly's & Letten's & Jeff's - old firms he remembered 'em still
And he'd crewed every' Crampin's Cricketer; all o' Consol's great soccer teams
Then wi' Northern's pride, & wi' Ross's Big Cats - he 'ad sailed wi' 'em, diesel & steam

He recalled the Remillo & Resolvo, the Clifton & the Northern Crown
The Bellona, the Barnett, the Bradman too, the Hondo & the Huddersfield Town
He recounted the pride & the glory when the trawling was in its prime
Wi' the Wolves & the Everton, the Grimsby Town - he'd sailed with 'em all in his time

In the Great War he'd fished in the North Sea; every trawler at war he could name
And the four hundred crewmen who lost their lives for the owners' reward & acclaim
When the Howe ran ashore on Bear Island, he was there at the rescue, he said
And he'd stood on the deck with a starvin' crew when the Sargon returned from the dead

Then he spoke of those early steam trawlers – the Aries & Zodiac too
When he said that 'ud be eighteen-eighty-three, well of course it was then that I knew
Though the stories he'd told were enthralling, I said: Dad, you've been stringin' me along
Then he fixed me with a stare, & he asked me: Where have the Grand Old Ladies gone?

I returned to the bar for a refill where I scowled at the barman & moaned
Sayin': That there old fella can spin some yarns! He replied: Aren't you drinkin' alone?
Of the old man I'd left in the corner not a sign or a trace could I see
But the walls still echoed his ghostly refrain and the names he'd recounted to me

THE GRAND OLD LADIES

Verse:
In the Al-bi-on one chil-ly eve-nin' I was warm-in' me-self by the fire When I
spied in the cor-ner an old fish-er-man, who I thought I'd en-gage to en-quire: If I
stood him a pint, could he tell me an-y trips he'd a mind to re-call? Well, he
gave me a wink, then he parked his drink say-in': Aye lad, I've sailed wi' 'em all. We

Chorus:
called 'em the Grand Old La-dies, That took us to the Arc-tic grounds. Here's a
trib-ute paid to the ships that made the trawl-in' trade go round, the trawl-in' trade go
round! Well he'd

THE THREE DAY MILLIONAIRES

Wave goodbye to your Daddy, his three days are done
And he has gone back to sea
Sailing on icy cold northern wastes
Catching fish for the landlubbers' tea

Chorus
Three days ashore, three days of fun
Chatting the lasses and drinking the rum
Don't look at the clock, the time goes too fast
The millionaire's time it is goin' at last

Millionaires they called us when we came ashore
After our three weeks away
With wages and settlings we'd rush to the pub
Like millionaires rushing to play

Cabmen and traders in our home ports
Loved it when we came to spend
Us millionaires rushing about on the town
Each week-day was like a week-end

You'd tend to the family, the wife and the kids
And bank a few quid out of reach
Then off to the pubs and the clubs with your mates
Sure you'd never land on the beach

We started with small boats, muscle and blood
The wind in our sails blowin' full
Diesel and steam took us further afield
Now our trawlers they rust in the pool

The good times are gone, the fine ships lie rotten
The big money we'll see no more
The memories we made will soon be forgotten
The millionaire's beached on the shore

THE THREE DAY MILLIONAIRES

Verse: Wave good-bye to your Dad-dy, his three days are done, and he has gone back to sea. Sail-ing on i-cy cold north-ern wastes, catch-ing fish for the land-lub-ber's tea. Chorus: Three days a-shore, three days of fun, chat-ting the lass-es and drink-ing the rum. Don't look at the clock, the time goes too fast. The mill-ion-aire's time it is go - ing at last.

CHAPTER FIVE

TRAINS AND BOATS AND PLANES

The prospect of war with Germany was now on everybody's minds. Being a port, Grimsby was seeing evidence of the build-up that would put the country on a war footing. Ships were being commandeered as soon as they had landed their catches. Towed to the fitting out jetties, stripped of all their fishing gear, they were converted to minesweepers, minelayers or escort vessels, depending on their size and tonnage. Men who had been without work during the depressed pre-war years were being taken on as tradesmen and labourers, extra to the complement of existing shore staff. The looming conflict, catastrophic though it was to be, created masses of work and overtime for all, so helping to ease the chronic unemployment problem at a stroke.

The politicians' minds now focussed on other issues. I remember the media reports about Neville Chamberlain stepping off the plane from Germany, holding up a piece of paper, the German peace agreement with Britain, waving his umbrella and announcing: "Peace in our time!" Whether or not his intention, it would give us a little more time to make ready, as Britain was a party to the Geneva Convention, which a few years before had committed us to a disarmament programme. We had practically nothing to defend the country with, so we now had to put our backs into it and show the rest of the world that we meant business.

A few months later Germany invaded Poland and Britain declared war on Germany. All the Territorials (reserves) were called up and sent to France to join the regular army there, the combined regiments being known as the British Expeditionary Forces.

One of my old mates and I decided to join the Local Defence Volunteers (later on to be re-named the Home Guard or 'Dad's Army'). In those early days our uniform consisted of an armband inscribed with the letters 'L.D.V.' worn with our civilian clothes, and we marched and trained with shouldered broomsticks instead of rifles. If Hitler's troops had invaded then, we would have faced them sternly with our broom handles drawn, then easily overpowered them as they rolled on the ground in helpless fits of laughter!

Still, we were doing a useful civilian job in the daytime and working many hours of overtime on top, reserving one night a week for our drills. Our commanding officer was Captain Falconer, a local timber merchant on the Alexandra Dock. We were making a contribution towards the war effort, and our consciences were clear.

But young lads like me felt we wanted to do more. When the disastrous retreat from Dunkirk became known, I heard on the grape vine that all the fitters, boilermakers, shipwrights and other tradesmen on the docks were to be declared reserved trades. I thought, "Now's the time for me to do something about joining up." But first things first.

As our air-raid shelter was still lying in pieces in the back garden, I decided to put it up that night with the aid of my brother Walt. We assembled the shelter in place, measured its length and width and pegged the dimensions out near the garden wall, then dug the hole to drop it in.

By the time we had dug deep enough, we were well below clay level and water started seeping. So I decided to dig a sump in the lowest corner, into which I could drop a pipe and attach a semi-rotary hand pump that could be operated from inside the shelter, taking the water out through an overflow pipe into the garden. All this I would fit after we had dropped the shelter into place. It was heavy and awkward to lift, so we had a bit of a struggle, but we managed it all right at the expense of a little sweat.

The following night after work we put a wooden floor in and built the bunks. Then I fitted the semi-rotary pump. It was a second-hand one that I'd bought, stripped and re-built at work in my dinner hour, and I'm pleased to say it worked like a dream – a new pump couldn't have done better. I patted Walt on the shoulder and said, "Come on kid, I think we've earned a drink." (He was big built and looked older than his years, so I could risk taking him to the pub.)

Over our pints I told him why we had put the shelter up in a hurry, but to keep it to himself. I had made my mind up to join up the following day. Walt was waiting for his ship to dock at Immingham, where he would join her as a galley boy, so he was doing his bit too. Later on he was to be on the dreaded Russian convoys. We had a good drink together, wished each other luck, shook hands and staggered home. He was a good brother and still is one of the best.

I had decided that I wouldn't tell my parents until I had enlisted. So I made my way to the Town Hall, which was the Royal Navy enlistment centre. The enrolment officer took all my particulars, including details of my experience as a marine fitter. He sent me to the first of six cubicles to be examined by the first of six doctors. I stripped off and he remarked on my fine physique for my size. After giving me a good check-up and pronouncing me 'A1' he directed me to the next cubicle. Well, I passed all the medicals until I came to the final doctor – the eye specialist. Directly above was a skylight through which the sun's rays were shining intermittently. Because of this I couldn't read the chart properly and he failed me. I protested about the light, but he wasn't impressed.

But I wasn't going to be beaten. Nursing my bruised pride I went along to the old Public Library, where they were signing on volunteers for the Royal Air Force. I hoped I might get a chance at air crew. Again I was required to go through a series of medicals, this time passing even the eyesight test. However when it came to the equilibrium and blood pressure tests I failed, so that put paid to any hopes of flying. Still, I was thrilled to find out that I had been accepted for training as a flight mechanic.

At last I was in the forces. First I was sent to Padgate for kitting out and square bashing. After passing out from there I had to go to Halton in Buckinghamshire for my fitter's training. It was an eighteen week course, and we were housed in proper brick-built billets. The workshops were enormous and the tools and tutors were very good, but everything came as second nature to me. I passed out 'L.A.C.' and received my first proper posting. I had been hoping to find myself going somewhere exotic. In fact, I ended up at Binbrook airfield – only twelve miles from Grimsby. Just my luck!

There were two squadrons at Binbrook: 12 Sqdn., equipped with Wellington bombers with twin Merlin engines, and 142 Sqdn., with Pratt and Whitney twin radials. I was seconded to 'A' flight of 12 Sqdn., and stayed with it until 1941.

One of my special planes was 'S for Sugar', its crew being all young gentlemen just out of their teens. The pilot was turned 21, and after doing twelve successful operations over Germany and France, he managed to arrange four days' leave to get married. When he returned we were making preparations for his next trip, destination Dusseldorf.

Whilst doing the daily inspection the young skipper called me over on the dispersal and asked me if we mechanics would like to go along to his crew's hut after he'd signed the form 700 (airworthiness certificate). He signed then we went down to his hut. There he took out a large biscuit tin from his locker, and removed the lid to reveal a layer of his wedding cake. He carefully lifted it out and, putting it on the lid, asked if we would join him in celebrating his marriage. This had been the wish of his dear young wife. Of course we accepted and in addition drank a toast to our skipper and his new bride.

Take-off time was ten o'clock that night, and it was my turn to see the planes out of dispersal to the perimeter track, where they had to line up with the rest of the squadron ready for take-off. I remember it was a beautiful moonlit night. The aircraft was waiting its turn on the runway; the bomb-aimer signalled the second pilot to open the bomb doors so he could check his load. This done, he climbed aboard. The skipper waved his arm for 'Chocks away!' and with an Aldis lamp signal from the watch tower 'S for Sugar' took off. She circled the 'drome once in the moonlit sky, as we crossed our fingers and prayed for her safe return, then we watched her disappear into the distance.

Next morning we watched the planes come in one by one. They all had some damage or other, so we knew they'd been through heavy flack. At about five-thirty we knew that all but three had returned. By seven we learned that two had managed to limp home to other 'dromes, but neither of these was 'S for Sugar'. We waited while ten o'clock to see if we could get any definite information. None came, and the aircraft and crew were pronounced lost or presumed missing. God rest their brave souls.

Eventually I reached the decision that I was becoming too involved with the crews privately as my close friends, and it was slowly breaking my heart as I counted my good young colleagues already dead. So I put in for an overseas posting, hoping also that there would be a better chance of volunteering for air crew. My posting at last came through for the Far East. But that was not to be.

I was again sent to Padgate for kitting out, this time with tropical kit, and then to Manchester to board a train for Gourock, from where we were ferried out to the troopship at anchor in the River Clyde just off Greenock. Incidentally I must express my deep appreciation for the wonderful hospitality offered by the marvellous people of Gourock, who supplied all the embarking troops with tea, sandwiches and cigarettes.

We embarked on the biggest ship I had ever been on. It was one of the North and East African liners, about fourteen thousand tons. We numbered approximately two thousand troops in all – Army, Navy and Air Force. We R.A.F. lads occupied the bottom mess-deck, with the Navy in the middle and the Army in the top, next to the deck. We were allocated hammocks slung across the mess-deck tables, and were to take turns as orderlies, regardless of rank. Without much delay we set sail to a destination unknown by any of the troops.

When we reached the Bay of Biscay we joined a convoy of ships escorted by a number of destroyers, about four I think. It was about that time, as I recall, that the numbers of diners on the mess-deck started to fall off. With (some) sympathy and much amusement I recalled my own first trip, but since I and a few others were never to be sea-sick, we made the most of the situation and began to eat like lords. There was one snag. As the tables were directly underneath the hammocks of the stricken sufferers, we had to keep scrubbing them down.

We encountered a great storm in the bay, but soon rode through it, and safely reached the Azores, where we were told of a change of plan. Though we still weren't informed of our intended destination, we were given the sad news that Singapore had been forced to surrender.

Our convoy then made its way to the Mediterranean, and when the tender came alongside at Gibraltar a few of the troops, including me and twenty-nine other airmen, were taken aboard. Twenty-five were transported to North Front, which was more or less a transit base for planes going farther east. I was one of the remaining five deposited at the seaplane base at New Camp.

My new posting was only a few yards from the Spanish border, and the nearest town was La Linea, but as Spain was supposed to be a neutral country there was a 'no-man's-land' area and a border patrol on each side. Quite a few Spaniards worked in Gibraltar, but a nine o'clock curfew meant they had to be over the border before that time or lose their passes.

Gibraltar itself was quite a small place, consisting of Main Street and Irish Town. There were two drinking houses in Main Street, the Cafe Universal and, just past the Governor's Palace, the Trocerdero. As you can imagine, these were both well patronised by all the forces of the garrison. There was also a lovely park filled with exotic plants, flowers and trees, reverently called Alameda Gardens, and it was a magical haven of natural beauty.

The Governor was the late Lord Gort, and a very strict ruler he was. Every man in uniform – including officers – had to salute as he approached the Palace and not drop his arm until he was past. Otherwise it was like peacetime in the town, all the shops lit up at night, no blackouts, and full of merchandise.

I joined 202 Sqdn., consisting of Catalina and Sunderland flying boats. These were anchored in the harbour on floating buoys, so whenever a plane had a major inspection it had to be brought up the slipway. To achieve this the mechanics would have to don divers' suits and boots, and wade out up to their necks to the aircraft to attach wheels. When these were secured the lads waded back, discarded their diving gear and were awarded their customary tot of rum. It was normal practice to be the guest of the tot glass after receiving a wetting, and if there happened to be a teetotaller amongst them, there would be an extra tot for the nearest lucky diver. It was real full strength Navy rum, and needless to say I often managed to get a second tot!

I was refuelling an aircraft one day when a big capital ship (which later on I found out was the King George the Fifth) came into the harbour from the commercial anchorage, to moor up at the detached mole, aided by six tugs. Of course it created quite a big wash. All of a sudden the plane I was on jumped up and down like a bucking bronco, and what with the metal on the wings being hot enough to fry an egg on, I lost my stability and fell headlong into the harbour!

What a glorious sight it was, although I had no idea that it was so deep! It was a very clean harbour, and I was able to see all the beautiful vegetation on the bottom in wonderful Technicolor. I was able to study the purply-blue Portuguese man-of-war, small octopi, and many other different coloured types of fish, on my way back to the top. I was picked up by the refuelling barge, and then went ashore in the motor dinghy for my tot of rum. I was only wearing a pair of khaki shorts and plimsoles, so I soon dried out. You'd be surprised though how many men slipped and plunged (accidentally) into those dazzling depths. And we got through a fair amount of rum.

My cousin Harold was a Royal Marine on the King George the Fifth, and Reginald Foort, the famous radio celebrity organist, was a seaman on board. His organ was kept in the Walrus hangar, where he used to give recitals to help boost the morale of the crew. He also played for dances when the ship was in port, on which occasions Wrens could be invited aboard.

Harold and his buddy came to visit me on the camp, and I got permission to show them round a Sunderland. I took them aboard the aircraft using a motor dinghy, and showed them how the depth charge racks were loaded from the inside before they were mechanically transported out under each mainplane. Each rack held four charges. The number carried in the storage racks inside was about twenty, and the system of loading and dropping the bombs on the unwary 'U' boats was very successful, as demonstrated by the number of submarines the squadron had sunk. Although as I told my friends, we were stationed in a very strategic position in the Straits of Gibraltar, and had a range of about one thousand and eighty miles up the 'Med' or down the east coast of Africa.

They were very interested in the protective armour that was carried, with as many guns as a Flying Fortress. This was necessary since the top flying speed was only eighty knots, so guns were the only protection. Full flying endurance was twenty hours, though they only ever flew for eighteen, so as to keep a reserve of fuel for emergencies.

After I had shown them the cockpit and controls, they were most impressed with the wardroom facilities for the crew members to take turns to rest on a long trip, and were amazed at the size of the aircraft. They thanked me and invited me aboard the 'K.G.5', subject to the permission of their CO. This was granted and I thoroughly enjoyed my conducted tour of this great warship, but was not very impressed with the living quarters, which seemed cramped for such a large vessel.

After completing my overseas tour I had a spot of leave. It was a great feeling walking down the street where my family lived. As I proudly strode with my kit-bag on my back, a joyful glow came over me to see the front of the house all decorated up with bunting, and a big sign in coloured letters declaring: "WELCOME HOME TO OUR SON".

That night Dad took us all out to the old Jubilee Club down Yarburgh Street. We had a right royal night there, all the local lads in uniform, and a few Yankee guests.

We really enjoyed the main artist, who was known as 'Our Erb' - a great local comic. Where he missed his vocation I don't know, because he was as good as I had ever heard on the radio. He was the type who created laughter as soon as he set foot on the stage. This particular night he was dressed as an ancient Briton, in an old bear-skin and wielding a great wooden club like a tapered tree-trunk! He brought the house down with all his topical ad-libbed jokes and jolly audience participation songs. He and other comedians in our area helped us through those difficult years. Though by now everybody knew that thankfully the war in Europe was nearly over.

I hadn't received my new posting yet, so while I was at home I thought I'd go down the docks to thank my workmates for sending me cigarettes and things while I was away. As I walked out of the fitting shop I met the gaffer, who shook me by the hand and told me that I would be welcomed back to work as soon as I was demobbed. On my way back down Corporation Road I called in to see my old friend Ron Reneichs for a glass of his sarsaparilla and a chat about old times. He had photos of all of us Marsh lads and lasses, now in the forces, who had used his teetotallers' club. Many a successful romance had blossomed in there, thanks to Ron's hospitality.

At last I received my posting by telegram. It was for Bottesford, an aerodrome between Newark and Grantham, in sight of Belvoir Castle. The aircraft flying out of Bottesford were occupied mainly in picking up stragglers from France, Holland and Belgium, and re-uniting them with their units in Germany. When I arrived I was taken to my billet, which was a Nissan hut in a field shared with a flock of sheep. It could have been worse – in the next field was a herd of cows!

There were twenty beds and lockers in the hut, and nineteen of these were in use. The one near the door being empty was mine, so I packed my kit in my locker and made my bed up and got myself comfortable. At about 1600 hours the lads started to arrive in ones and twos, and I made myself known to them. They were a decent lot and we were soon to become friends and comrades. They were in their late teens and early twenties, and full of spirit. They hadn't actually been called up – at that time there was a system of training young men as reserves, for fear there was trouble anywhere else. Towards 1946, the war in Germany being over, they weren't likely to see action abroad.

For me things were back to normal, with one exception. For I soon found out that I was to be in charge of this great set of lads, and responsible for the hut and its contents. It had a door at each end, a big coke-burning stove in the middle, a coke scuttle, sweeping brush and shovel, a squeegee, floor polish and polisher. (The lino flooring had to be kept highly polished).

My first job was to make out a duty roster for room orderlies. Every man was responsible for his own bed space, and the orderly for the rest. Each bloke took his turn fairly, everyone pulled his weight and it was a very happy billet. We were all issued with pushbikes because it was so far from the airfield itself. However the railway station was just outside the camp – very handy if you wanted a night out.

For our entertainment we had the wonderful city of Nottingham. What a welcome us British lads used to get there – we were honoured guests wherever we went. There was free food and drink for us at the railway stations, the buses were free, and the girls (who were as pretty as you'd find anywhere) were always reluctant for us to spend money on them.

My usual drinking companion was a tall dark young man from Market Harborough who had the next bed to me in the hut. His name was Des Robinson – 'Robbie' – a very quick learner, I was bringing him up into the job so that he could get his ranking, and very soon we became real pals.

One night it seemed that the hand of fate had touched me as Robbie and I were rolling out of a pub called The Hand And Heart (situated on the Derby Road side of Nottingham Castle). Robbie said, "Let's chat up these two young lasses, John," nodding towards a pair who were walking on the same side.

"Don't forget we've got a train to catch, Rob," I said. "It's gone ten o'clock already."

Well, we got talking to these two very pretty girls, and I asked the smaller one, who had told me her name was Clarice, if I could see her again. That was the start of our great romance.

After a few meetings Clarice told me that she was a war widow, her paratrooper husband having been killed in September 1944 in the landings at Arnhem. I was flabbergasted when she told me she had four children, comprising a girl of eleven months, and boys of three, six and nine years.

Although I had fallen for the tender trap, I was no fool, and knew I had to think very carefully about what responsibilities I would be taking on if we were to be married. So I decided to go home at the weekend to talk it over with my parents.

Dad took me out for a pint and wished me all the luck in the world, but warned me that it would be a different kettle of fish with Mother, who was dead set against me marrying Clarice. On reflection I thought, "What the hell, I haven't even asked her yet – she might not even want me." We loved each other very much but she also loved her children. If she accepted my proposal, she would have to move away from her family and friends in Nottingham, not knowing whether she would receive the respect she deserved in Grimsby.

So it was a dilemma for both of us. But after talking things over at length and weighing up all the pros and cons, we decided to give it a go and set the date for the wedding. Going over the details Clarice had to divulge a fact that no young woman would want to disclose – she was four years older than me, twenty-eight whereas I was just twenty-four. But I didn't mind. She was as pretty as a picture, with lovely rosy red cheeks, strawberry blond hair and always with a cheery smile. No wonder I wanted to spend the rest of my life with her!

Obviously with my free time now being taken up with serious courting and wedding preparations, my nights out with the lads became fewer.

I was working late on the 'drome one night, and Robbie had gone out on the town with another young airman. I had just turned in at about eleven o'clock when the doors of the hut flew open, and I could hardly believe my eyes and ears at what happened next. Robbie, obviously well into his cups, held the door open while his equally drunken mate drove about fifty sheep into the hut! You can imagine the uproar – beds tipped over and muck everywhere. It was a right shambles!

I fortunately escaped most of the mayhem as the flock went past my bed and down the middle of the hut to be let out of the door at the other end. When it was all finished, I made them get the beds all squared up and told them, "You'd better get up at five in the morning – I'll set my alarm clock, and I want you up! Either that, or I'll have to put you on a charge." Given the choice, they settled for the early morning call. They'd to clean the hut up, re-polish the floor, and repair any damage done.

Five o'clock comes and the first awake was Robbie. I told him to wake the others, and made them see to their proper chores first, cleaning their buttons and boots for parade, then they got their overalls on and got cracking cleaning the hut up. Afterwards they could go for their washes and showers and have their breakfasts.

They were good lads – in an hour, it was all done. They even washed the windows, and everything was spick and span. They'd made a good job of it, and I congratulated them. They in turn said how grateful they were to me for not putting them on a charge. I told them to let it be a lesson to them, and not to let it happen again. "No, it won't, it won't."

Not much!

The next weekend they went out and came back in the same condition as before. It was the cow field this time. They all thought they were at a rodeo, betting each other which cow they could ride. They were getting hold of their horns and trying to mount, and of course ringleader Robbie succeeded. He got on one and rode it right round the field. So one of the others opened the gate and said, "Come on, ride it through the hut!"

Robbie said, "Not on your bloody life, you know what John said last time – we're definitely on a charge if we do anything like that."

Anyway I came out of the hut to see what was going on, as they were making a hell of a row, and I yelled, "Come on, get in the hut, all of you. And get off that cow Robbie!" As he tried to, it bucked him and he finished up in the ditch. You've never seen such a bloody mess in your life!

Fortunately neither he nor the cow was hurt, and from the embarrassed look on his face I think he'd learned his lesson. Suddenly sober now, he blurted out an apology, slunk off to get cleaned up, and we all had a chuckle at his expense.

I had an embarrassing experience myself one night. I was returning to Bottesford after visiting my fiancée, had just caught the last train and dozed off. (I'd had to walk all the way from Stapleford to the station and it was quite a hike.)

The train stopped and I awoke suddenly, thinking I'd reached my destination.

Without thinking, I threw open the door and jumped out – and dropped about twenty foot! We weren't at a station, but stopped on an embankment near an army camp a few miles before Bottesford. Some soldier, needing to get back to camp before he was locked out, must have pulled the communication cord. I thought I'd broken my legs – I was bloody crippled! It's not very pleasant, when you're expecting just to step out onto a platform, to take a surprise fall like that instead.

As I lay there dazed, up come the guard and engine driver, looking for the guilty party. And of course, who do they grab hold of? But I still had enough about me to convince them of my innocence, and they helped me crawl back into the carriage to recover. While they were doing this, we could see the real culprit running over the fields and off into the distance – back to his camp. I won't tell you what I thought of him!

A few weeks prior to my wedding I took Robbie to see my fiancée and her family and have tea with them at Stapleford. In the evening we went out to the local club, had a game of bingo there, and I sang them a few songs from the stage. We stopped fairly late and of course it came to the time where we'd missed the last bus. And by the time we'd walked all the way to the station, the last train had gone as well. So I told Robbie that I would hitchhike back to camp – I'd done it a few times before. He thought about it for a moment, and then declared, "I'm not. I'm too knackered. I'll sleep in the Grantham train."

This train had been shunted into the siding, awaiting the early morning London run via Grantham, stopping at Bottesford on the way. He'd already got his ticket, and he asked one of the porters, who said that it would be all right. So Robbie settled down in one of the carriages while I thumbed it back to camp. No problem.

The next day I had to be on the flight early, so I didn't see Robbie arrive in. About mid-morning the Flight Sergeant in charge called me over.

"John, there's a telephone call for you!"

It was Robbie. He sounded anxious. "Is that you John? What the hell am I going to do?"

"Why, what's happened? Did you get on the wrong train?"

"No, I got the right train. Trouble is, I didn't wake up and missed the stop at Bottesford. In fact I slept through quite a few stations."

I wondered why I hadn't seen him that morning. "Well, when did you wake up then?"

He muttered (very embarrassed), "When the train hit the buffers – at King's Cross!"

I had to think quickly. Technically he was absent without leave, which could have serious repercussions. I told him to see the Station Warrant Officer at King's Cross, and get him to make out a warrant for the next train back to Bottesford. Then I went and explained the situation to the Engineer. He was sympathetic, and when Robbie finally got back to camp at three that afternoon, all he'd lost was a day off his leave.

He was usually lucky like that. But he was a likeable bloke – perhaps that's why people were willing to make allowances when he got into scrapes.

At last the day came when I got married at Stapleford Parish church, and Robbie was my best man. He took me for a few drinks beforehand, but I think he needed more Dutch courage than I did! He was a bit sweet on one of the bridesmaids but I don't think anything ever came of it.

I was posted to another station soon after that, and lost contact with Robbie. It was a conversion unit at Cottesmore, near Melton Mowbray. We were on four-engined Halifax bombers, converting pilots from Wellingtons to go out to the Far East. Conversions consisted of circuits and bumps (practice landings). About every four or five bumps we fitters had to check to see if any damage had been done to the planes.

When the crews had completed their daytime flying course, they went onto their night training. It was very hard work for all concerned, and we were practically living on the dispersals, at times eating and sleeping there.

From Cottesmore I was sent to a 'drome in Somerset, called 'Merryfield' by the Yanks. They had Avro-Yorks, big four-engined troop carriers. At that time they were airlifting wheat to India, which was suffering one of the worst famines it had ever known, and we were maintaining the engines. There were two squadrons of about eighty aircraft.

Taunton was the nearest town, along with Ilminster and Axminster. But being newly married, I was of course on my best behaviour, so I didn't go out much with the lads. Anyway I wasn't there long before being sent to Cardington to get demobbed, which is exactly the opposite from joining up.

First you have to pass the doctors, then hand in your kit. Next you are measured and supplied with a shirt and two loose collars, collar studs, a three-piece suit, shoes and socks, as well as an overcoat and a trilby hat. Then I went to the accounts to receive my pay and gratuities, and collect my railway warrant. The war behind me, I swaggered to the station with my trilby on one side, just like Humphrey Bogart, good and ready for Home Sweet Home!

JOHN EVARDSON

A BOMBER'S MOON

He was a rosy-cheeked young pilot, who'd be twenty-one quite soon
They were going out on ops that night, & theirs was a bomber's moon
Coming up to twenty-three hundred hours, on a night in August forty-one
And the lads all eager for Dusseldorf, their target yet to bomb

Now the rosy-cheeked young pilot had got married the day before
And he'd shared out his wedding cake from its box on the Nissen hut floor
Ah but now he revs the engines, while the aimer checks his load
And he waves an arm for 'chocks away!' then taxies up the road

He taxies onto the runway, while us ground crew give a sigh
As we watch our aircraft's silhouette, 'gainst a moonlit, Binbrook sky
We mutter a prayer for the crew aloft to 'give old Jerry hell!'
Ah, but in our hearts our only wish is to see 'em back safe & well

Six o'clock next morning, & they're drifting home to land
They're directed back to dispersal by their ground crews' guiding hands
But 'S' for Sugar's ground crew scanned the sky till ten o'clock
And then silently went back to their beds, that wouldn't need a rock

Maybe you're shot down o'er Dusseldorf, or drowned off the coast of France
Or maybe yet you're safe, but then we've learned the laws of chance
So rest in peace all you young men – you're heroes through & through
More young stout hearts will take your place to make up a bomber's crew

A BOMBER'S MOON

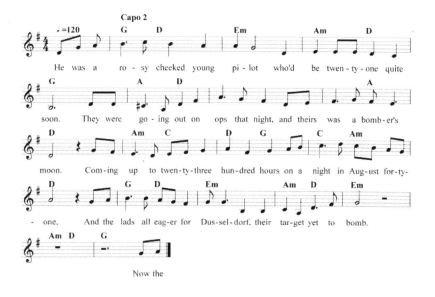

Capo 2

He was a ro - sy cheeked young pi - lot who'd be twen - ty - one quite soon. They were go - ing out on ops that night, and theirs was a bomb - er's moon. Com - ing up to twen - ty - three hun - dred hours on a night in Aug - ust for - ty - one, And the lads all eag - er for Dus - sel - dorf, their tar - get yet to bomb.

Now the

NO MAN OF MINE

Chorus
No man of mine shall go to sea
And risk his life for someone's tea
To toil in constant jeopardy
A hostage to the gale
To haul for shoals where ice is king
In hopes of riches home to bring
And leave his family worrying
No man of mine shall sail

When I was five, my Mam & me
Went down to wave Dad off to sea
Not knowing he would never be
Returning home again
My brother John was brave & strong
And proud to be his father's son
But when he said: I'm signing on
Our Ma she told him plain:

Twas in the dance hall by & by
A handsome young man caught my eye
He smiled at me, though he was shy
And asked me up to dance
His shiny shoes, his hardened hands
His pleated suit & baggy pants
Betrayed him as a trawlerman
So I coldly said: No chance!

Twas then that he turned on the charm
And said one dance could do no harm
So I got up & took his arm
Enchanted by his smile
My heart was young & knew no fear
As fortune called me down the years
And I forgot my Mother's tears
When we walked down the aisle

With lonely nights I've had to pay
The weeks my husband's been away
Then when he's home, such happy days
And he's a skipper now
But we've been favoured, he & I
And when my sons declare they'll try
A spell at sea, well that's when I
Recall my Mother's vow

NO MAN OF MINE

No man of mine shall go to sea, and risk his life for some-one's tea, To toil in con-stant jeo-par-dy, a host-age to the gale; To haul for shoals where ice is king in hopes of rich-es home to bring. And leave his fam'-ly wor-ry-ing; no man of mine shall sail! When I was five, my Mam and me went down to wave Dad off to sea, Not know-ing he would nev-er be re-turn-ing home a-gain. My broth-er John was brave and strong and proud to be his fa-ther's son, But when he said: "I'm sign-ing on," our Ma she told him plain: No

JOHN EVARDSON

NEVER TELL A TRAWLERMAN 'GOODBYE'

As he stops and rests his kit bag at the door
In the stillness while his taxi's standing by
You can say: 'See you next trip love' – nothing more
For you never tell a trawlerman 'Goodbye'

It's hard to face an icy winter's morning
When he's off to brave the Arctic sea and sky
You embrace him while he's shivering and yawning
But you never tell a trawlerman 'Goodbye'

> Chorus
> When the Humber takes his trawler out to sea
> When you see him off, you do it silently
> With a smile, a kiss, a cuddle and a sigh
> But you never tell a trawlerman 'Goodbye'

The day he sails can't be your washing day
You'll have to put it off, however dry
There's a danger you'd be washing him away
So you never tell a trawlerman 'Goodbye'

Don't think about the dangers of the trawling
He's got to go, so keep your chin up high
He doesn't want to see your teardrops falling
So you never tell a trawlerman 'Goodbye'

> Chorus

There's only one 'Goodbye' for trawlermen
Don't speak or let him see it in your eye
Say a silent prayer he'll come back safe again
But you never tell a trawlerman 'Goodbye'

> Chorus

NEVER TELL A TRAWLERMAN 'GOODBYE'

CHAPTER SIX

THE FITTER ON THE SHORE

Arriving at Grimsby Town Station I was greeted joyfully by my young wife Clarice who, never having seen me in civvies before, at first didn't recognise me. My immediate task was to get my name down at the local Housing Department for a council house. An ex-serviceman and family were allotted their place on the housing list by means of a points system. You were awarded points for years of service, number of years overseas and number of children. Your present living conditions were also taken into consideration. As we were living with my sister (and she had children of her own) we were allocated a house almost at once.

When we had settled in I decided to approach my old firm for my job back. This should have been a formality, as it had already been promised me. I went to the time office window with my cards and received my time book and firm number, which was seven. This was a Monday morning, so I went and stood in line in the fitting shop with the rest of the outside fitters, waiting for the foreman to come round with the work requisition sheets for the various ships. I was amazed when he gave out all the work and left me standing there like a dummy!

I couldn't complain to Mr. Gidley as he was on his holidays. So I decided to take the bull by the horns, and now being a man of few words tackled Herbert Bye directly. I demanded to know what I'd done to deserve such treatment, and reminded him that the gaffer had told me to report for a job.

He gave me a bad-tempered look. "I am the gaffer while Mr. Gidley is away. To speak man to man, I don't bloody well want you. It's through such as you getting demobbed that my lad has been called up for national service. Now bugger off!"

My temper got the better of me. Being fit and strong I lifted him off the ground by his coat lapels growling, "That's not my fault and you know it. Besides a spell in the forces isn't going to hurt him. In fact it'll make a bloody man of him."

He stuck to his guns. "I don't want bugger all to do with you. You can do as you like. You're one of the sods that have wangled their way out, so my poor young lad has to go in."

I was boiling. What he said was completely untrue. Just as I was about to really lose my cool, Les Howse appeared behind me and took me by the shoulder saying, "I'll give you a job in the fitting shop with pleasure Jack. I can use a fitter with your skill and I know you'll enjoy the work. What do you reckon?"

Les, gentleman that he was, had saved the day and I was happy to accept his kind offer. Really though I'd got no choice.

I remained in the fitting shop for two or three years and did a lot of good jobs, and nobody could doubt that.

By now I had resigned myself to the fact that life for Clarice and me wasn't going to be a pushover. As a family of six we had to forego all the little luxuries that other people were now beginning to enjoy. I became a workaholic, not just because I liked the work, but because I needed the money, and weekends off were something of a treat.

Eventually Herbert Bye passed away. I didn't hold any grudge against him, in fact he had done me a favour, God rest his soul. At least in the fitting shop you were working in relative comfort most of the time, away from the exposed bitter weather conditions on the North Wall.

Old Harry Perry took over then as outside foreman, and he was a real good bloke. He came up to me as I was working at my bench and said, "I didn't care for the way Herbert treated you when you got demobbed a few years ago, and I hope we can now right the wrong that was done. I know what some of you lads went through during the war. I've a young nephew who saw a lot of action and was unlucky enough to be blinded."

(This young hero was to become a very clever and well known physiotherapist at Grimsby General Hospital's special unit on Springfield Road, Scartho, despite his own disability.)

And so due to Harry's kindness I began to take on outside work again.

After a time the old gaffer, Mr. Gidley, passed away following a short illness. This came as a big shock to everyone. He had been a good friend to us all. The great man was succeeded by another very good engineer, Mr. Percy Greenaway, who resigned his position as head engineering tutor at the Grimsby School of Technology in favour of this more satisfying position.

We used to get one or two perks as engineering fitters. A tot of rum, a can of beer and some Old Friend tobacco plus papers for rolling; and perhaps a few packets of fags from the skipper. The charge hand fitter would share them out down the engine room. These little gifts were never refused – that would have been a great insult. They were hard earned for jobs well done, and we knew that the sweat and toil we put in was much appreciated by the crews. We worked long hours, and used to lose all track of time as we gave of our best under a tight and limited schedule. If you were offered the least little tit-bit you accepted it with both hard-worked scruffy hands, because wages were small and every little handout helped.

I used to wonder why the tradesmen of our great little country, at that time turning out top quality products for the rest of the world, applying their high-grade technical skills in peacetime as they had in the war, were still treated like dirt by the chinless wonders who were in control. I believe that was the start of the downfall of many of our once great industries. Firms were being run on a shoestring, with no profits being put back in for new or modern machinery. No wonder so many old established businesses have since disappeared, all because of the greed of a few.

Most of the get-rich-quick merchants are now on the dole themselves. Some however managed to make their pile. I know of one individual who didn't have the guts to fight in the war, yet had the nerve to go out to the Middle East when the fighting was over, and collect and sell all the scrap metal left over from the conflict, making himself a millionaire overnight. That's life I suppose.

There were a few consolations for the ordinary working man. Grimsby's pubs were still thriving, just as they had done before the war. Some nights after work I would drop in at the Saracen's Head on Cleethorpe Road. The pub was also known as 'Tommy Taylor's' – after its landlord, a well-known character. He was the only publican I ever knew that gave his regulars a drink at Christmas and on his birthday.

I used to enjoy a game of darts in those days. Once Tommy says to me, "I'll have a little bet with you, Jack. If you can get three darts in the bull, there's a cigar and a pint for you."

Well, you won't believe it, but not only did I get three in the bull, but each one went in the end of the one before! Tommy was amazed. He spluttered, "That doesn't count. But I've never seen it done before. It's a bloody miracle. You can have two cigars and two pints an' all. But wait while I go and get my camera." And if they hadn't fallen out before he returned, I'd have been able to show you a photograph of my marvellous achievement!

The Saracen's was renowned as a meeting place for the fishermen when they were in dock. Tommy's back room was always jam-packed with skippers and crews holding forth with stories of their latest trips, and the little bar rightly earned its knick-name, 'The Skate Pound'.

Tommy and I would team up in there for games of fives and threes, taking on teams of fishermen, and we proved to be an unbeatable combination. I used to have that many pints waiting for me behind the bar through winning games of dominoes that my drinks never cost me a penny.

While playing, we'd be entertained by the trawlermen's tales of what they'd got up to at sea. This was where they told of the hazards they'd faced in the freezing Arctic conditions – for at home with their families they'd never complain about their arduous lives. They were real men, mostly the last of generations, of Nordic origin whose history was dominated by the constant battle with the sea. To them, though the risks were real (as was too often demonstrated by the many ships and hands lost over the years), danger was a part of their heritage and destiny. They accepted it.

There'd be crewmen come into the pub straight from sea, sea-bags and all, and into the Skate Pound for a jar, with tales of the gigantic shoals they'd got amongst. Or what the skipper had been up to. They'd probably put into a Norwegian port and been out on the town with the local lasses – you'd get all the juicy details!

You won't find the Saracen's there now of course. Like so many other good pubs, it's gone. It stood opposite to where the Albion is now.

I suffered from warts at one time. My hands used to be covered in them. I had a big one on the back of my hand and whenever I used a hammer and chisel it used to bleed like hell. This old watchman says to me one day, "Eh Jack, do you want me to get rid of them warts for you?"

I replied, "I'd do owt to get rid of 'em."

He says, "If I tell you what to do, will you believe in it and do exactly what I say?" I nodded, then listened carefully to his remedy. "Go to the shop and buy a lemon, and cut it in half. Get a real mother of pearl button, put it in a saucer, squeeze the juice of the lemon onto the button, then leave it while the morning. In the morning put half the residue from the pearl button onto the biggest wart on your hand, and at night before you go to bed put the rest on the other warts. Keep this up until you see a difference."

So I did as he'd said. A week later I said to my wife, "Have you found anything in the bed?" She said she hadn't. I showed her my hands. They were absolutely clear. Not a wart was left – and they never returned either.

Now I'll tell you about the time the R.N. generator ran away with me. It was about 1959, and the ship was the Real Madrid, the first diesel trawler at Consol's. She had Mirrlees 8 cylinder 4-stroke engines, built by Mirrlees, Bickerton and Day of Stockport. Our firm was the first to fit them to trawlers, as they were usually used for bigger vessels. They had to be governed down a lot, but the extra power was there if needed.

I'd got the requisition sheet for this ship, with a couple of other fitters. We had to remove the main engine exhaust valves and inlet valves, clean them up and put them back again, check the injectors and re-set the tappets – well, that's all routine. Also on this R.N. diesel water-cooled generator, we had the pistons to take out along with the piston liners, which had an outside rubber ring on to keep them water-tight. You took the big ends off the crankshaft, pulled them through with a length of rope (after taking all the tops off the rocker boxes), tried the crankshaft for wear, and checked the angle of the crankshaft webs that the big end was on, to see that there was no twist.

I got all this done, and it would be about five o'clock at night. I says to my mate, "Right, Sandy, it's about time to run it now. Get it all boxed up. Will you top the air intake up while I go on deck and have a smoke? You know how to do it, don't you?"

There was a mesh filter in the air intake, and underneath that was wadding. The air intake had a round top secured by a wing nut, and there was a mark on the outside telling you how much oil to put in. When you filled it up to that mark, the wadding soaked up the oil you'd put in, and the level just came to the top of the wire mesh then.

"Yes, of course I do," he said.

I left him to it and went up for my smoke.

When I came back down I asked, "Are you all ready then?"

He nodded. I put my foot on the air start valve, opened the valves up, letting the fuel oil into the injectors, and off she went first time. Beautiful. We checked it for leaks and everything and she was going lovely. We were feeling very satisfied with a day's hard work well done, and ready to shut her down.

All of a sudden she picked up speed. And picked up speed. And picked up speed.

I started to panic a bit. "What the hell have you done Sandy?"

"I don't know Jack. What have *you* done?"

I said, "All I've done is fitted new pistons and liners." Then a thought occurred to me. "How much oil did you put in the air intake?"

"You told me to top it up, so I did. I filled it to the top."

I went cold. I'd heard of a fitter making the same mistake. The generator had fed off the excess oil in the air intake and reached such a speed that the flywheel had come off and gone straight through the ship's side.

"Bloody hell!" I roared, as the generator was still gaining speed at an alarming rate. A flywheel is thick, solid, and weighs over half a ton. To get to the air intake I had to pass within a hair's breadth of the still accelerating flywheel.

It was now or never. My heart in my mouth, I darted past it and whipped the top off the intake, flinging it to one side.

At first nothing happened. I was terrified, for now I was in the direct path of the massive flywheel if it should come off. There could be no escape for me. Then at last the engine began gradually to slow down, but we had to wait a full half hour for it to stop. When it had I said, "Unpack the tools. We'll be working nearly all night now."

"What for?"

"We'll have to re-check the tappets, valve stems, push rods and everything." I had to go through all the procedure I'd been through that day, and fortunately all the spare parts we needed were available in the stores. We did very well to finish at half-past-nine that evening.

The following morning I had to go and report to the Superintendent Engineer, to tell him that we'd worked late, and why, fully expecting a bollocking. But instead of being angry, he congratulated us. He had a leather cigar case in his pocket, and he took it out and offered me one.

He said, "You did a thing there that I never would have thought of. And then you had the common sense to strip that engine down again after the extensive run it had had. And you probably saved the ship." Then he got his whisky bottle out, and we had a tot together. It just goes to show that it's not always the best fitters that get the foremen's jobs.

Here's another little episode that bears that out. We were working on a trawler one day on the fitting out jetties. We had to strip the main engines, pumps, steam dynamos, boiler mountings and winch engines down for their regular Lloyds insurance surveys. It was a major overhaul and about six fitters and mates were used on these projects.

One of these young fitters was employed in dismantling the centrifugal water end and steam engine for inspection. The centrifugal was a circulating pump that circulated sea water from the main injection through the condenser and over the side through the main discharge. This cold sea water condensed the exhaust steam from the main engines, was pumped by the air pump and transferred through the main check on the boiler front, and back into the boiler. All the engines on the ships were made mainly out of cast iron. I don't know if you know this, but salt water revolving at speed in a casting causes an electrical charge, which draws the actual metal out of the casting leaving plain carbon, just like black lead, which can be scraped off in lumps.

Well this fitter (who shall be unnamed) removed the inspection cover and stuck his carbide lamp in to have a look around. There was such an almighty explosion that could be heard at the end of the jetty, and the big casting lay on the platform in a great heap. It was a miracle that nobody was hurt.

The explosion had been caused by the gases that had accumulated inside from the corroded metal. The young fitter should have known better, and he was certainly learning the hard (and costly) way. Later when Harry Perry the foreman retired, he got his job, maybe to keep him out of mischief – who knows?

Not all the incidents were quite so serious. Once one of the lads parked his bike right alongside the ship, against a lamp-post on the jetty. When it came time for him to go home for his dinner he looked for his bike and couldn't find it anywhere. He hunted all over for it.

A quarter of an hour went by and I asked the watchman if he'd seen anyone take the bike. He said, "To tell you the truth Jack, I'm not supposed to let on, but he's such a little rogue they thought they'd play a trick on him. Look up that foremast."

The bike was stuck right on top of the mast. They'd hoisted it up there on the jiltson wire. I said, "Go and tell him." We lowered his bike down for him and he was that glad to get it back he never said a word about it.

Some of the painters were a rum lot. If it was good weather and you hung your coat outside on one of the fair leads or on the casing and the painters were around, they didn't shift your coat – they just used to paint round it. A similar thing happened when the riveters were fitting a new plate on the focs'le. I saw a bloke hang his coat on a hook. They put this hook back, and instead of hanging his coat on it, they put a rivet through one of the button holes into the plate. When he came to get his coat, he had to cut a hole out of it before he could put it on to go home! They were up to all sorts of tricks like that.

'Scrumpy' was what the painters called the brown stuff they put on when they were graining. This happened whenever a ship went for a fit-out. After putting the undercoat on, they used to grain all the casing side, which made it look smashing. An ordinary painter would put the brown undercoat on, then one of Consol's two 'artists' would follow up with the scrumpy work. Or what we used to call 'cat's arseholes' – because that's what their artistic flourishes reminded us of. To achieve the required effect they used a special duck-hair brush.

Well, a new artist had been set on, and one of the young fitters decided he'd play a trick on him. He got the artist's tin of scrumpy and mixed in some dog dirt with it, until it was nice and brushable. Then he returned the tin to where the artist would pick it up. The new artist went to work and there was no immediately noticeable difference.

Then steaming day came and the lovely artwork was subjected to the heat from the engines. The aroma was like nothing else you've smelt in your life – it was bloody horrible! The poor artist came round, put his hand to his nose and said, "I wouldn't sail in this ship for a bloody pension!"

One of the old fitters was that mean, he wouldn't go out and buy a tin of varnish. He'd been begging that much paint off the painters, they decided to teach him a lesson. One day he took an empty treacle tin to one of them and said, "Will you fill this up with varnish for me? I've just got to finish a door off at home." The painter took the tin down below, and passing the food store happened upon some real treacle. When the old chap came back to work the next morning, after a summer evening's painting, he was moaning, "There's fifty million bloody flies stuck on my living room door!"

The painters used to use 'prams'. A pram was a flat boat – more like a raft – that they used for pulling themselves along the ship's side while they painted it. One day the fitters wanted to cart their gear over from one ship to another one that was anchored on the other side of it. As the lorry couldn't get round, they decided to 'borrow' the painters' pram. They pulled it to the side of the jetty. They chucked a load of chains, toolbags and whatnot into it.

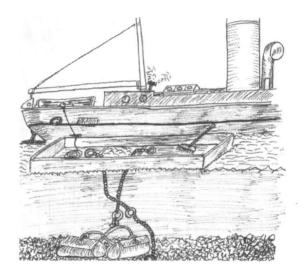

Unfortunately they didn't realise that only the ends of a pram have boards – the middle has none at all. This is so that the painters, while scrubbing a ship, can dip their long-handled scrubbing brushes in the water. So, in fact all the fitters' gear was going straight through the pram to the bottom of the dock! When they got over to the other ship, they looked for their bags and chains, and of course, there weren't any. One of the labourers said, "Well I know we chucked 'em in there." With that, he stepped out onto what he thought was a board and ended up going for a swim instead. When he'd been fished out, they had to send the divers down to retrieve all the lost gear.

The young foreman I mentioned earlier, now he had the authority, took an unqualified dislike to me and, as well as stopping my overtime, started giving me all the shitty jobs. Lining winch drive shafts up and things like that, and at that time the coal ships used to have to go under the coal drop and be coaled. The bunker lids were each side of the winch where the driving shaft was, so you'd be laid down there while they were dropping these big two-ton coal buckets. Of course the coal would be going all over you while you were working on the shaft bearings. When you crawled out you looked just like a bloody crow. And if there was a steam pipe burst in the bunker, you used to have to rig your own platform up, dig all the coal away and try to do the job in filthy, cramped conditions. My labourer soon got fed up of this treatment and left, but I was more stubborn. I was a good diesel as well as a steam fitter, and the rate of pay for diesel work was equivalent to time and a quarter on steam work. So he stopped all my diesel work too. I hadn't given him any cause for this treatment, as I was well known as a good tradesman and was greatly favoured by my old foreman. Perhaps it was professional jealousy.

He never liked me, although he'd been apprentice under me, and I'd taught him all I could. He was a bit of a dunderhead, and now that he was foreman we were dire enemies. He used every dirty rotten trick in the book to try and get rid of me, but I was made of tougher stuff than that. I could take all he threw at me, and I always 'kept my nose clean', as the saying goes.

I told him one day, "I'll meet you coming down the ladder as I'm going up." My prophesy came true years later. Later when the firm folded up, he took a job at Humber Graving Dock, Immingham. He didn't last there long – he got the sack after a week for incompetence. He finished up on the road as a travelling salesman, but I sometimes wonder whether he even had the brains to hold that job down.

Soon the effects of the extreme working conditions, whether from the normal course of the job or from the mucky work that was now being handed to me, together with the long hours of sheer hard graft, were to take their toll. I was suddenly struck down with pneumonia and pleurisy, which kept me on my back for eighteen weeks. I was very ill, but while recovering had time to reflect on the poor rewards I was reaping in exchange for a lifetime's dedication and loyalty.

When I eventually returned to work, it was to face the same treatment as before, if not worse. For now my labourer had been taken from me and not been replaced, so I had to do all my own fetching and carrying, big hammer work and all the rest of it. Now I had to do all the dirty jobs with no assistance whatsoever.

I'd stood about a month of this diabolical treatment, as I was (and still am) very strong-willed. I'd always been used to keeping any personal troubles to myself, but I suppose something was bound to happen to stir me into action.

One morning he'd made out the paper for work on a diesel ship and, thinking the fitter concerned was off ill as he hadn't turned up for work, he grudgingly gave it to me. I wondered if things were taking a turn for the better. I took the paper and got started on the job, looking forward to a satisfying day's work.

When I'd got the engine stripped down, the engineer's runner came aboard and approached me nervously. I sensed something was wrong. "What's up?" I asked.

"Don't take it out on me Jack, I'm just doing my job. The foreman's sent me." (He daren't come and tell me himself.) "Tommy isn't sick – he's just arrived in late – and he'll be on board in a minute to take over. You've got to go on this steam fit-out." With that, he thrust the paper in my hand and turned tail.

I was furious. All the frustration and anger that I'd been nursing were ready to explode. I knew it was no good trying to talk rationally with this foreman – I'd tried before and failed. Besides, I was afraid I might do something I might regret later, however much satisfaction it would have given me to plant one on him just then.

My only recourse was to the Superintendent Engineer. When I got to his office I hadn't cooled down at all, so I ended up having a row with him. I regret that, for he was a decent fellow who had always respected me. I tackled him over the difference in money between steam and diesel work, and how the younger fitters who only knew diesel were taking home more money than the older hands who could handle either. I asked him what he intended doing about it.

Quite rightly he told me I should take it up with my union, who had negotiated the rates with the firm. Of course, as we older fitters were in the minority, the union couldn't care less about our problem. We'd approached them before, and as long as the majority of members were happy, they didn't want to know. All I could do was issue the Super with a personal ultimatum.

I said, "I'll give you a month. If something isn't done by then, I'm leaving."

He smiled. "You'll not do that Jack, you've been here too long. "

"There's no need to laugh about it gaffer," I scowled. "This is my bread and butter I'm talking about."

"We'll see," came his reply.

One week went by, two weeks, then three weeks came, and things were getting worse for me. I was earning such low money through lack of overtime that I wasn't able to support my wife and family, and I was getting into debt. By the time the month was up, I thought, "It's now or never."

Seeing that I was beaten at every turn, I went to the Super's office and told him it was no longer a viable proposition for me to use my hard-won knowledge and skill for other people's benefit in return for a pittance. I had a sick wife and a growing family, and everything cost money.

I was bitter and my mind was made up. He didn't have much to say. Really there was nothing he could say. I left him and went to the time office for my cards and back pay. As the wages clerk made up my money, he said he was surprised I hadn't done it months earlier, after the way I'd been treated. So I took my cards and money, packed my tools, then got on my bike and rode away from the docks, leaving the job I had loved for over thirty years.

THE FITTER ON THE SHORE

When I was just a little lad
For workin' folk, the times were bad
And jobs not easy to be had
In Grimsby, Lincolnshire
While still at school, Dad says to me:
Will yer tek a pleasure trip to sea
With your Uncle Alf, you know that he's
A trawler engineer

To be a fitter was my dream
Enthralled to see the power of steam
Make man & steel a mighty team
I'd found a course to steer
My eagerness soon found reward
I built a bike in our backyard
Dad says: If you can graft that 'ard
You'll mek an engineer

I learned from masters of their trade
To see no ship should be delayed
And worked like hell to make the grade
As war was drawin' near
Then I joined up & took me kit
Like millions more I did me bit
And when I came out I was fit
To be an engineer

A faulty pump, a lazy winch
To raise the vacuum just an inch
From dangers we must never flinch
No situation fear
Except to see our trade decline
And idle trawlers moored in line
That'll send a shiver down the spine
Of any engineer

How proud I was to make that trip
A crew of men & a trusty ship
And when the third hand caught the whip
To winch the cod-end clear
The mate below untied the knot
And the crew all cheered the prize they'd got
But they never would have reached that spot
Without their engineer

A store-lad first down on the docks
At the counter I'd to use a box
Just four foot seven in me socks
And in me fifteenth year
The first two years they quickly passed
An apprentice fitter then at last
So eager to be learnin' fast
To be an engineer

From steam we went to diesel oil
In sleet & snow on deck you'd toil
Then down below where blood could boil
The heat was that severe
For trouble-shootin' men were we
To get the trawlers back to sea
While skippers scowled impatiently
And blessed the engineer

But at fifty-odd you've had your day
And ruined your health for your lousy pay
Then it's: Thank you Jack, now on your way
It's time to pack your gear
    Far off those glorious days of steam
As you sign for their retirement scheme
Still proud that you fulfilled your dream
To be an engineer

Chorus
The trawler engineer at sea
The fitter on the shore
For shame that we should never see
Such craftsmen any more

THE FITTER ON THE SHORE

Verse:
When I was just a lit-tle lad, for work-in' folk the times were bad, And jobs not eas-y to be had in Grims-by Lin-oln - shire. While still at school, Dad says to me: "Will yer tek a pleas-ure trip to sea, With your Unc-le Alf, you know that he's a trawl-er en-gin-

Chorus:
- eer?" The trawl-er en-gin - eer at sea, the fit-ter on the shore. For shame that we should nev-er see such crafts-men an - y more. How

129

DOWN DOCK NO MORE

I was just a lad first time me Dad took me with him down dock
To see the grand old ladies proudly glide in through the lock
Then came the day he called me from my bed at six o'clock
For the start in life that I'd been waiting for
From store boy to the fitting shop, I had to wait me turn
Then apprenticed for a fitter, I was keen watch & learn
Till I knew me way round engine-rooms & trawlers stem to stern
But I won't be going back down dock no more

Chorus
No I won't be going back down dock no more
To the cold Pneumonia Jetty & the hard nor-easter's roar
To the sweat & toil & the greasy oily overalls I wore
No I won't be going back down dock no more

I loved the work, I loved the ships & soon I'd served me time
I knew those grand old ladies when the fleet was in its prime
Some nights I'd cross the lock pit gates & hear the midnight chime
I was young & there was overtime galore
Through rain & wind & sleet we toiled to turn those ships around
Well fit to face the dangers of a deadly Arctic ground
And the freezing hell that beckoned where those mighty ships were bound
But I won't be going back down dock no more

The race was on to win the fish, for the grounds were teeming then
With the biggest landings since the old 'uns could remember when
Two days for us to fit 'em out, then turn 'em round again
Like a frenzied game, with no-one keeping score
Their skippers drove 'em hard, resolved to bag the lion's share
Some sailed 'em into waters where a sane man wouldn't dare
They'd trawl the depths of Hades if they thought the fish were there
But I won't be going back down dock no more

We had our years of plenty & I earned some decent pay
But it broke me heart to watch our giant industry decay
It was greed & over-fishing brought us where we are today
Like rotting hulks we're beached up on the shore
There's nothing left of trawling now – the men & ships are gone
The lathes are still, the tradesmen's skill the lads relied upon
And the years of wasted wisdom I won't pass on to me son
For I won't be going back down dock no more

DOWN DOCK NO MORE

CHAPTER SEVEN

HAPPY LANDINGS

Feeling alone and dejected, I rode along the top of the Humber Bank towards the new chemical factories. I passed Titan's and Courtauld's till eventually I came to a little factory at Stallingborough, smaller than its two giant neighbours. Something seemed to draw me towards it, so I rode down the bank, past the big sign that read "Doverstrand Ltd. Latex Division", and through the factory gates.

I thought, "This could be just the job for me." If the money was good it would suit me, and at least I'd have peace of mind. I parked my bike and tools and went into the reception block, where a pleasant young lady asked if she could help me. Thinking that the best plan would be to go straight to the top, I asked her if I could see the Chief Engineer. She asked me my name and trade and got straight on the blower to him. "Yes, Mr. Townsend will see you now. Second office on the right."

Mr. Townsend didn't waste time. He asked me where I'd worked. When I said that, apart from wartime service, I'd spent all my working life at Consol's on Grimsby Docks, he just said, "When would you like to start? We can double the basic wage you were earning there, and there's as much overtime as you want to work. You'll find we believe in paying for a tradesman's skill here. I hope you'll agree to join our little family."

Well I stayed with Doverstrand until I retired early due to ill health – a legacy from my life on the docks – and I can't express how happy I was there. It was a chemical plant, obviously different from a trawler engine room, but it was thoroughly absorbing and fascinating engineering work. I made many new friends and found out what it was like to work for a really appreciative employer.

The children brought us much joy over the years. Tom, the eldest, won a place from grammar school to join the R.A.F. technical college at Halton in Buckinghamshire. Chris became a control room technician at Courtauld's Humber bank factory. John served his apprenticeship at Humber Graving Dock at Immingham as a marine engine fitter, later to become the youngest chief engineer to graduate from Grimsby, working on the big deep sea trawlers. Sheila began her apprenticeship at Burnett's printers, only leaving to get married (to a fine fisherman, George, who later took a shore job with Doverstrand). David, our youngest son, qualified as a Certified Accountant with Laporte's, another Humber bank chemical company.

So all in all, though it's not all been plain sailing, I think Clarice and I haven't made a bad job of bringing up our family. Now I'm retired and we are living our lives simply with all the memories of forty-odd happy years together. Happy years of nostalgic realism, some good, some not so good. The good is that I still have my first love, dear Clarice, and the company of our grown-up grandchildren.

The not so good part is that I had to retire early at fifty-nine owing to ill health, with crippling arthritis, high blood pressure and angina. I am sixty-seven now and still find retiring gracefully the hardest task I've ever tackled.

And I would happily do it all over again. I consider my life to have been a great success, having started from small beginnings. Though I must admit, earlier on the thought did cross my mind, "You bloody fool, you'll never do it." I did though, and surprised a lot of people, including my mother. Perhaps one of my greatest regrets is that we couldn't see eye to eye on such an important matter.

So, what did I achieve? Well, if nothing else, I fulfilled my boyhood ambition to become an engineer, and I've seen many different aspects of the trade during my varied career. My greatest love, steam, is now all but gone completely and will soon be lost forever. That's progress I suppose. But the great fishing industry that spawned all those dock trades has gone the same way.

Some blame our politicians and foreign fleets – and they certainly didn't help – but I believe it was unbridled competition and overfishing that stripped the grounds bare, sending ton upon ton of surplus fish to the fertiliser factory and leaving nothing for future generations.

But the fish will return one day. Let's hope when that happens the industry will revive, but with improved controls and more respect for conservation.

Then perhaps a new batch of youngsters will have their chance to take up careers in maintaining the trawler fleets, taking pride in their trade, earning a living wage and truly enjoying 'A Fitter's Life!'

THE NORTH WALL

I went down dock this morning, where I used to earn me pay
And walked by empty berths, where deep-sea trawlers used to lay
Where we fitted out their engines, the diesel & the steam
But their mighty power is gone, & now they're just an old man's dream

> Chorus
> And I know with each new generation everything must change
> Of the good things we once took for granted not much now remains
> But I ask the rain that rattles all along the bleak North Wall
> Could they not have left a little? Did they have to take it all?

We hadn't long to turn them round, for the fishing mustn't stop
And when new parts were needed, then we'd make them in the shop
They were glorious grand old ladies – I wish someone would explain
Why they're scrapped, or half way round the world, & won't sail home again

I've drunk me share with trawlermen, with hands as hard as nails
All risked their lives for small rewards – some perished in the gales
But they were only casual labour, signing on from trip to trip
So they got no compensation when they were signed off their last ship

When the Dogger Bank was flourishing, it was plundered night & day
Not a thought for conservation, for there were shareholders to pay
And not content with plenty, competition knew no bounds
Private enterprise prevailed, & finished off our fishing grounds

Now all I've left are memories of the diesel oil & grime
And the mucky, damp conditions that made me old before me time
Though the memories aren't all bitter – for there were good times after all
But I think I'll not return again to that empty, bleak North Wall

THE NORTH WALL

SONGS FROM A FITTER'S LIFE

A companion CD, containing re-mastered original recordings by The Little Band of most of the songs in this book, is available from the Editor, David Evardson.

E-Mail: david.evardson@btinternet.com

Telephone: 01472 693137

Proceeds from sale of the CD to be donated to St Andrew's Hospice, Grimsby.

10674536R00079

Printed in Great Britain
by Amazon